FREED TO SERVE

Also by Michael Green

Acts for Today
Baptism
The Empty Cross of Jesus
Evangelism through the Local Church
I Believe in Satan's Downfall
I Believe in the Holy Spirit
Matthew for Today
New Life, New Lifestyle
To Corinth with Love
Who is this Jesus?
Why Bother With Jesus?
You Must be Joking!

For Timothy and Sarah
and their generation of servant leaders

CONTENTS

PREFACE TO THE NEW EDITION

It is gratifying, and surprising, that a book published thirty years ago should have been continuously in print and is now in need of a new edition. Why should this be?

The answer, I think, lies in the radical examination it offers of crucial matters which in the past have been taken for granted in the life of the Church, but in these days of massive cultural change require a fresh look. I wrote the first edition of this book when my son was a small child. He is now a highly innovative missionary overseas. He has had to learn a new language, a new lifestyle, new patterns of thought, new expressions of the faith. The Church in the West is attempting to do just that, but is often tempted – by fear, tradition, or cultural pressure – to stray far from the principles enshrined in the New Testament. That is sad, because these principles are so powerful and effective when they are given a chance.

The book was written originally for the Lambeth Conference in 1968 which was going to give attention to the nature of the Christian ministry. In those days the clergyman was, as it were, the apex of a triangle: everything in the church was under his control. There was agitation for women's ordination, but no action was taken. There was talk of lay ministry, but there was not much of that either in your average Anglican church. The issues of the day were clerical issues. Was the 'threefold ministry' of bishops, presbyters and deacons really the only expression of Christian leadership that should be recognised? Was a ministry derived by supposedly unbroken succession from the days of the apostles really necessary for a church? Was the celebration of the Holy Communion a sacrifice which only priests could make? Those were the things they talked and wrote about extensively in church circles in those days. And all the time the sixties revolution was transforming secular society and its attitudes, while the people of God occupied themselves with matters like these, fiddling while Rome burnt. And burn it did. For the next three decades the fall-out from the mainline churches escalated enormously, averaging at a thousand people a week. It has taken years to settle down. Even now growth in Christian churches in the West is at best spasmodic and far from widespread.

So often in those days church services were highly predictable. In the mainline churches there was a minister, an organist, a choir and a Sunday School. That was the staple diet, with various additions. But change was in the air. The charismatic movement made enormous strides in the sixties and decades which followed. It has become the most significant of all influences on world Christianity. And in the goodness of God it made a great deal of difference to the Anglican Communion for whom this book was originally written. No longer do you find Christians arguing much about whether or not the Holy Communion is a sacrifice. No longer do you find ordination through hands purporting to go back to the apostles a critical factor in evaluating ministries. No longer is the ordination of women a far off 'maybe': it is here to stay, and is increasingly appreciated. No longer is the vicar seen as the only serious minister in the church: the concept of every member ministry is widely accepted (though not yet widely enough). No longer is the worship in a great many churches dominated by the organist and a choir, robed and paid. More often than not there is a small orchestra, a singing group, and a variety of spiritual songs being used alongside hymns to express the joy and devotion of the congregation. Indeed, no longer do the mainline churches continue as if only they had a licence to operate. Many of the most committed members of their congregations, fed up with waiting for change and renewal, deserted the mainline churches. They started house churches, which soon outgrew the houses which gave them their name and became the new church networks which are a dynamic part of Christianity in Britain today.

So it is a very different situation today from that in which this book first took shape. Why, then, should it be necessary to republish a book like this? Because we still have a very long way to go before most churches get back to a dynamic biblical set of priorities. That is why.

We need to recognise the massive contrasts which Chapter 1 highlights between the idea of Christian ministry to be found in the New Testament and that which prevails in most churches. We need to recapture in deed, not just in word, the revolutionary model of leadership given by Jesus – that real ministry is serving and facilitating others, not bossing them around. We desperately need, in this last decade of the millennium, to grow thousands of churches which are missionary through and through: congregations which are reaching out to the unchurched all around us. This can never be done by the clergy alone: only by churches where all members see themselves as ministers of Christ and act accordingly. The strict division between clergy and laity is neither biblical nor helpful for a church full of ministers. We need to admit, when Pentecostal churches worldwide have grown from nil in 1900 to 190 million today, that however fussy some of us may be about apostolic succession, threefold ministry and sacrificial priesthood, the Holy Spirit does not seem unduly troubled about them. And we need to make room for both men and women complementing each other in Christian leadership. Jesus and the apostles gave an enormous thrust in this direction and we need to follow that.

All that and more still needs to be taken on board by churches that want to grow, but there is another issue, and it is addressed in the last two chapters of the book. How can one help a church to grow from the old monolithic view of ministry to the biblical, cooperative one? How can people in a congregation be equipped for ministries of many different kinds, so that the Church corporately begins to express in society at large some outlines of what the Kingdom of God might look like? How can the body of a church be enriched by the contribution of many living cells, groups meeting in homes under lay leadership for companionship, prayer and service? Those chapters emerged from years of work in churches that did move in the direction of every member ministry. It was an enormous privilege to be part of St. Aldate's, Oxford from 1975 to 1987 and of Holy Trinity, Vancouver from 1987 to 1992.

I hope this new edition of *Freed to Serve* will encourage many others who are struggling with questions of Christian leadership to move from the model of the manager to that of the servant, from solo leadership to every member ministry, from the self-relating church to the missionary congregation. If it does that, this new edition will be thoroughly justified.

Michael Green
1995

A STUDY IN CONTRASTS

There are few aspects of Christianity which need a more radical reappraisal than the purpose and function of its ministry, if we are going to be obedient to the call and commission of Christ in a fast-changing society. The trouble is twofold: we are disobedient to the directions Christ has given us about ministry, and we are failing to meet the needs of contemporary society. We are missing out at both levels.

Consider the image of the Christian minister in the modern mind. It is perhaps a bit better in America where there is a high level of churchgoing and a great deal of vital Christianity, but in many parts of the Western world the image is deplorable. Christian ministers are thought irrelevant to ordinary life. They are simply there to be called on in crises, or to utter pious sentiments for the rites of passage we go through. They are involved in protests and petitions. They keep ancient buildings going, and adjust the thermometers which signal the growth of building funds. They recite services on Sunday, but nobody knows what they do for the rest of the week. They are figures of fun, feeble men or forceful women, attempting to teach Christianity to middle-class adults and children, but steering clear of the real world. They seem to be, and

often are, unsure of their role in a society which
finds them an anachronism.

If Christian leaders are on the whole not very successful at relating to modern society, they are even
less successful at implementing the teaching of the
New Testament on Christian ministry. There is no
single area where we have departed more signally
from the indications given in these foundation documents of the early church. Here are a dozen or so of
the more obvious contrasts.

1. *In the New Testament, ministry had to be received
before it was exercised.* You had to let Christ serve you
before you attempted to do anything for Christ. Simon
Peter learnt this lesson at the foot washing. He was
most indignant at the suggestion that Jesus should
wash his feet: thoroughly embarrassing. But he had to
learn that unless he allowed Jesus to wash his feet he
could have no lot or part with him. This passage (John
13:8ff) enshrines the first basic principle of ministry in
the New Testament. None of us can serve Christ until
we first let Christ serve us. We all have to undergo
the humbling, embarrassing business of being washed
and cleansed by Jesus. Until then we are useless. But
in most churches of the Western world it is perfectly
possible to get yourself ordained without having had
any vital experience of the cleansing of Christ. You
can become a minister of the grace of God without
ever having experienced it. No wonder such ministry
is ineffective.

2. *In the New Testament, all Christians were called to
ministry, not some.* That is astonishing to us! We have
grown used to the idea that there are the ordinary
Christians, who sit in the pew on Sundays, and the
extra-special Christians who become missionaries or
clergy or nuns. Somehow they are different. They, and

not the rest of us, are the ones called to serve. When we think of Christian ministry today we instinctively think of people ordained to the ministry of the word and the sacraments. So you either are a minister or you are not.

It was very different in New Testament days. They knew nothing of any such distinction. All Christians are called to serve Christ, all are commissioned for ministry. We shall be looking at this further in a subsequent chapter. It is, to our shame, sufficiently revolutionary a concept to need further expansion. But for the moment it is sufficient to emphasise that for the New Testament writers the Christian ministry is coextensive with the Christian church.

3. *In the New Testament, ministry was a function, not a status*. It was a verb, not a noun. We have got ourselves tied up in talk about indelible character in ordination and the like: they spoke of the need by love to serve one another, to bear one another's burdens and so fulfil the law of Christ. Jesus had drawn the contrast between the world's ideas of leadership and his own. 'The kings of the Gentiles exercise lordship over them . . . But not so with you; rather let the greatest among you become as the youngest, and the leader as one who serves . . . I am among you as one who serves.' (Luke 22:25–27) It is not the status of the agent but the nature of the action which constitutes Christian ministry.

4. *In the New Testament, ministry was something corporate and shared*. With us it is nearly always exercised singly or at best in pairs. We never find a presbyter in the singular in the New Testament. A presbyter is always a member of a team. This was true of the apostles themselves; the twelve functioned as a team, and they set up local leadership in the same way. We refuse to follow their example, and then complain

3

because our minister fails to be omnicompetent. This is a serious situation. It is bad for ministers to be made to feel they are on their own. It may lead to despair, arrogance, blindness to the realities of a situation, or inhibiting the gifts of others. It is bad for the church members. They may well become critical and lazy. When the different limbs in Christ's Body are not allowed to exercise their God-given ministry, they are harmed and their gifts atrophy. Team leadership is much harder to achieve, but much more fulfilling for one and all when it is achieved. It is, moreover, as we shall see later on, practical politics in any church, however small.

5. *In the New Testament authorisation followed ministry rather than preceded it*. We tend to think of ministry as something exercised in and for the church only after proper authorisation. The early Christians saw all ministry as a gift from the ascended Christ for his Body through its members; the authorisation followed once the member had shown evidence of having received the gift. If we think about it at all, we assume that the ordination will convey the gift. All too often it does not!

6. *In New Testament days, character, not intellect, was the most important condition*. If you look at the qualities laid down for those who would exercise oversight in Christian assemblies (Titus 1:5–9; 1 Tim. 3:1–13; 1 Pet. 5:1–5) you will find that they do not concentrate on passing examinations and collecting an adequate amount of book learning. Instead they are much more concerned with the person's maturity: self-control, quality of family life, the ability to shepherd others humbly and tenderly – these are the criteria by which a candidate was assessed.

7. *In the New Testament, they selected their leadership from people of experience*. No novice was considered.

4

A Study in Contrasts

We ordain young people with little experience. We pay comparatively little attention to the morals of candidates. Provided they pass their college examinations, they can be drinkers, bad tempered, greedy, morose and solitary: there is still room for them in the ordained ministry. The selectors do not even interview spouses or families, let alone discover whether or not the candidates are able to manage their own family life before being put in charge of the family of God. And practically no attempt is made to find out whether or not the candidate enjoys a good reputation among unbelievers – something the early Christians found important.

This is of course because we see the ordained ministry as a career structure. Should we be doing anything of the sort? Is ministry much to do with books and memory, as we emphasise? Or is it more a matter of life and people, as the ancients thought? The question is at least worth asking. It affects training fundamentally.

8. *In the New Testament, people were trained on the job as apprentices, not in a college.* To be sure, colleges were not available to them. But college training did not come in until the nineteenth century. Was nobody properly trained until then? In the New Testament days, and for much of Christian history, people were trained on the job, in the fires of controversy, in the stress and strain of life. We take young people away from their natural milieu into semi monastic institutions based on secular models, give them book learning for three years, and wonder why they find it hard to fit in when we return them, not to their own area but to some quite different part of the country.

9. *In the New Testament, leaders were of two kinds, local and circulating.* The local ministry consisted of

5

presbyters or bishops or shepherds (all, it seems, synonymous) assisted in administrative tasks by deacons, male and female. It might well contain men or women with outstanding gifts in prophecy, exorcism, healing or teaching. The circulating ministry would consist, in the early days, of the apostles and prophets moving round from place to place, evangelising, setting up churches, encouraging them and seeking to maintain their unity. Apostolic delegates like Timothy and Titus continued this role, which in the second century devolved upon the newly emerging monarchical bishops. But not only on them. We still find in the third and fourth centuries itinerant teachers, theologians, evangelists and prophets moving round the churches in an encouraging and supervisory function, enlarging horizons and preserving catholicity. It would appear that the effective combination of the settled and the mobile ministry might still have a great deal to offer the church.

10. *In New Testament days, local ministry consisted of people called to serve and lead in their own locality.* It did not consist of ministers from outside the community who came in for a spell of years and then departed. Once again it is not hard to see the value of the local person, well known and respected in the local community, exercising the leadership of the local church in the company of other leaders, one or two of whom might well be from outside, so as to stimulate fresh ideas.

11. *In New Testament days, leaders were normally not paid.* They generally exercised a 'tent-making' ministry, thus solving at a stroke the financial problems that often today centre round the leadership of the churches. Of course, they might on occasion be paid: St. Paul contends eloquently in 1 Corinthians 9 for the principle that this could be proper: but equally

eloquently he makes it plain that he rarely availed himself of the privilege of being supported by the churches he came to serve.

12. *In the New Testament, the leaders saw theirs as an enabling ministry.* This is rare today. When an ordained man comes to a church he expects to do a great deal of the work. The congregation expect that he should. It is the exception, rather than the rule, to find him exercising a ministry of equipping the saints for the work of ministry, as Paul put it in Ephesians 4:12. The leader's task in the early church was not to do all the ministry himself, but to help other members of the Body of Christ to find out what their contribution to the service of the whole should be, and then do it.

13. *In the New Testament, doctrine was important.* Two qualities were looked for outside the character qualifications we have already glanced at. Candidates must be 'apt to teach' and must be noted for 'holding fast the faithful word'. They must be sound in the apostolic faith and competent in helping others to understand it and live by it. Nowadays, in contrast, one can be ordained in most denominations with the haziest notions about the existence of God, the deity of Christ, the role of scripture or the way of salvation. And people are ordained from some of the theological colleges without having ever preached a sermon under supervision, let alone having spoken on closed-circuit TV, or to a non-captive audience in the open air or taught in a school or on a factory floor. The ability to communicate is not rated highly in our training institutions. Is it any wonder that ordinary people regard the church as not for the likes of them?

14. *In the New Testament, ministry was seen in terms of people, not buildings.* Naturally, that is how we would all like it to be today. But the fact remains that many clergy are condemned to be the custodians of ancient

buildings with insufficent resources for their upkeep.
As a result, most of their effort inevitably goes into
upkeep rather than mission. The whole thrust of the
ministry in the early church, when they had no buildings to maintain, was flexible and designed to build up
congregations so that they could grow and spread the
gospel elsewhere. Mission is nowadays in bondage to
maintenance.

Of course it is proper to ask in what way we are
entitled to turn to the New Testament for guidelines,
so different were the people of the first century both
historically and culturally from ourselves. We could
not, even if we would, return to their situation. Their
preoccupations – circumcision, meat offered to idols,
and women's heads veiled in worship – are not ours.
Not that those New Testament issues have nothing
to teach us: they have. The abiding principles of
equal acceptance of all believers before God, of
refusal to compromise with evil, and of modesty in
dress, remain to guide us when the circumstances in
which those principles found flesh and blood in New
Testament days have faded away. But we should be
foolish to look to the New Testament as a blueprint
for 'the ministry'. For one thing, those pages tell
a story of staggering diversity. Congregationalists,
Presbyterians, Episcopalians, Brethren and Roman
Catholics can all point to some element in ministry
in the New Testament as justification for their own
brand of ecclesiastical policy. Pentecostals can find
all they need in Acts and 1 Corinthians, and Quakers
can turn with some propriety to the Johannine corpus
where no form of ordained ministry is apparently
envisaged. For another thing, the New Testament
does not give the impression that nothing should
be done for the first time. On the contrary, most
of the advances in definition of specific ministries

recorded there seem to derive from the needs of the situation rather than from any preconceived normative plan; for instance, the appointment of the seven, often called 'deacons' in Acts 6, the initiatives for the first missionary journey in Acts 13, the appointment of presbyters in every city evangelised in that journey (Acts 14:23) and the establishment of the Apostolic Council in Acts 15.

No, if we are prepared to take the scriptures seriously as foundation documents of our faith, it does not mean that we shall follow them slavishly irrespective of context and culture. But it does mean that we will face the challenges and opportunities of our own generation with a good deal more attention to the precedents afforded by church history, and the principles and precepts of the New Testament from which we have so markedly turned away.

Let us begin at the fountain head, go back to Jesus Christ, and see if he gives us any guidelines for Christian ministry.

2

THE MODEL FOR MINISTRY

If there is one word to sum up the ministry of Jesus, it is this: service. His whole ministry was one of service. This is apparent from the general tenor of the Gospel narrative, and from many specific utterances. 'The Son of Man came not to be served but to serve, and to give his life as a ransom for many' he told his followers. As he took the way to the cross, he made it clear that service was to be the hallmark of all Christian ministry. In contrast to worldly rulers, preoccupied with status and authority, 'It shall not', he said, 'be so among you; but whoever would be great among you must be your servant, and whoever would be first among you must be slave of all.' (Mark 10:43, 44)

This lesson of the royalty of service must have been imprinted indelibly on the minds of the disciples by what happened at the Last Supper. In the Middle East feet quickly get hot and dusty, and it was the job of the household slave to wash them. At the Last Supper there was no household slave.

None of the apostles was willing to lose face by doing the slave's job; so they sat with unwashed feet. We can imagine the amazement when Jesus rose from supper and laid aside his garments. Wrapping a towel round his waist, he began to wash their feet (John 13:4, 5). He was introducing them to a revolutionary idea of greatness – measured in terms of service. Relentlessly he pressed the point home. 'Do you know what I have done to you? You call me Teacher and Lord; and you are right, for so I am. If I then, your Lord and Teacher, have washed your feet, you also ought to wash one another's feet. For I have given you an example, that you also should do as I have done to you. Truly, truly, I say to you, a servant is not greater than his master; nor is he who is sent greater than he who sent him. If you know these things, blessed are you if you do them.' (John 13:12–17)

There is, I think, a hint in St. Luke's account that this action of Jesus arose out of a quarrel among the disciples over precedence and status. Although he does not record the foot washing, Luke does tell us of this devastating question which Jesus asked them at the meal: 'For which is the greater, one who sits at table or one who serves? Is it not the one who sits at table? But I am among you as one who serves.' (Luke 22:27) Once more Jesus makes it crystal clear that what is true of him must be true of his disciples. 'The kings of the Gentiles exercise lordship over them . . . but not so with you; rather let the greatest among you become as the youngest, and the leader as one who serves.' (Luke 22:25, 26)

The Christian church has found this a very hard lesson to swallow. Almost all consideration of church unity revolves round discussions on the validity of ministerial orders, their regularity, their authentication and their apostolicity. That is very natural. It is the way of the world. But it is not the way of Jesus Christ. He saw ministry not in terms of status but in terms of function. The pattern he set was the pattern of service. Of course, the very word 'ministry' means 'service'. But for Jesus this was no idle euphemism. It is no accident that the term 'ministry' is used to describe the whole of his public life and work. He was supremely and in everything the Servant of the Lord. That was his glory. He looked for no other. And so it must be with any ministry which claims to be truly Christian.

Jesus the Servant

How did Jesus come to think of himself in this light? He found it in his Bible, particularly in Isaiah 40–55. Here it is made very plain that the whole nation of Israel was called to be the Servant of the Lord; service is the corollary of election (Isa. 41:8–20). The particular elements of service which God looks for are obedience (Isa. 44:1; 65:12), witness (Isa. 43:12) and endurance (Isa. 43:1–6). But the nation refused to obey, recoiled from suffering and, instead of witnessing to the Lord, gave way to idolatry. And so the task of the Servant of the Lord devolved on a faithful remnant within Israel who accepted its implications. In the four Servant Songs of Isaiah (Isa. 42: 1–4; 49:1–6; 50:4–7; 52:13–53:12) the great themes are obedience, witness and endurance. The Servant is utterly obedient to God's voice (Isa. 42:1; 50:4,5), witnesses both to the lapsed in Israel and to the Gentiles (Isa. 49:6) and suffers ignominy and pain (Isa. 50:5,6). Indeed, though innocent, he bears the sins of the people (Isa. 53:6,11,12) and God accepts his sacrifice and vindicates his cause (Isa. 53:10–12).

We may never know how the prophet thought his words would be fulfilled, but it is certain that Jesus saw in them the foreshadowing of his own ministry. At his baptism the voice from heaven addressed him as 'My beloved Son, with thee I am well pleased' (Mark 1:11). These words are a composite citation of Psalm 2:7 and Isaiah 42:1. Jesus, the messianic son, is hailed as the Servant of the Lord in whom he is well pleased. The point is made equally emphatically at the outset of the fourth Gospel, where Jesus is greeted by the Baptist as 'the Lamb of God who takes away the sin of the world' (John 1:29, 36). This title would, of course, have taken the Jewish hearers back to the sacrificial system they knew so well. But it would have done more. It would have pointed the perceptive among them to the Suffering Servant of Isaiah 53, for *talya*, the Aramaic word for 'lamb', is also the word for 'servant'.

The three themes of utter obedience, fearless witness and innocent suffering, which marked the Old Testament understanding of the Servant, run through the ministry of Jesus. And so when at Caesarea Philippi Peter made his great confession that Jesus was the Messiah, the long-awaited deliverer of Jewish expectation, Jesus 'charged them to tell no one about him' (Mark 8:30). If they were thinking in terms of status and position they were entirely missing the point. So Jesus reinterpreted Peter's confession. He would not allow the term 'Christ' or 'Messiah' which suggested earthly pomp and military might. Instead, he joined together two utterly diverse concepts, and in effect asked Peter to see him in terms of them. 'He began to teach them that the *Son of Man* must *suffer* many things and be rejected.' Oscar Cullmann[1] was not exaggerating when he wrote:

Son of Man represents the highest conceivable declaration of exaltation in Judaism; *ebed Yahweh* (the Servant of the Lord) is the expression of the deepest humiliation. This is the unheard-of new act of Jesus, that he united these two apparently contradictory tasks in his self-consciousness, and that he expressed that union in his life and teaching.

The concept of the Servant was never far from Jesus's mind, as can be seen by a whole page full of references and allusions gathered by Joachim Jeremias.[2] Moreover it clearly became the dominant theme towards the end of his ministry. By word and deed Jesus demonstrated that he was fulfilling the task of the Servant to the bitter end (Luke 22:37; John 13:4ff; Matt. 26:28). Peter understood this (1 Pet. 2:21ff) and so did Paul (Phil. 2:6,7). Both of them, in fact, make specific reference to Isaiah 53. Two of the early speeches in Acts refer to Jesus as God's Servant (Acts 3:13,26; 4:27,30) and there are other New Testament allusions, such as Romans 15:7–12. Naturally, this title gave way to others, more comprehensive, after his resurrection, notably 'Lord': but it cannot be denied that the prevailing pattern and supreme glory of his ministry was service. It was, therefore, entirely in character when Jesus knelt to wash the disciples' feet. The Servant of the Lord had shrunk from the nation of Israel, from the faithful remnant, to a single person who fully embodied the vision. Later, that ministry was to expand again in his followers. Their ministry was to be marked by service.

The church of the Servant

Jesus is *the* Servant. He is *our* Servant. None of us can be a Christian, let alone a Christian minister, until we let Jesus be our Servant. As we have seen, Peter rebelled against so humbling and embarrassing an encounter with Jesus the Servant. But he learnt his lesson, and his first Letter is full of the theme of the Servant. 'Submit' is the word that comes again and again; it is applied to husbands and wives, to young and old, to slaves – and to Christian leaders.

In 1 Peter 5:5 he uses a rare word for '*Clothe yourselves,*
all of you, with humility.' It recalls the way in which
Jesus took a towel and girded himself. It is Peter's
way of saying that the church must be like Jesus.
It must be the church of the Servant. Christian life
begins when we allow Jesus to be our Servant. It
continues as, incorporated into Christ, we share the
role of the Servant which he made so much his own.
Of course we cannot share in the Servant's atoning
work. He and he alone took responsibility for the sins
of the world. But we can and must make his pattern
of ministry our own. Indeed, he commissions us to
do so. That is plain from the two mission charges to
the twelve (Mark 6:7ff) and the seventy (Luke 10:1).
We meet the same characteristics of service that we
saw in Isaiah and in the life of Jesus. They are to obey
the instructions of Jesus in going out on his mission.
They are to bear witness to the kingdom of God by
preaching, healing and casting out demons. And they
are to be prepared for suffering and rejection. Their
ministry is, in fact, an extension of their master's. It
is conceived in the same terms, be it for the twelve
or the seventy. For apostles and for church alike the
pattern is the same. 'In the kingdom, service is not a
stepping stone to nobility,' observed T.W. Manson:[3] 'it
is nobility, the only kind of nobility that is recognised.'

As the counterpart to this, Jesus warns his disciples
against the preoccupation with status and succession
that bedevilled the Jewish rabbinic schools. 'They love
the place of honour at feasts, and the best seats in
the synagogues, and salutations in the market places,
and being called rabbi by men. But you are not to
be called rabbi, for you have one teacher, and you
are all brethren. And call no man your father on
earth, for you have one Father who is in heaven.
Neither be called masters, for you have one master,

the Christ. He who is greatest among you shall be your servant.' (Matt. 23:6–11)

Such is the pattern for ministry set by Jesus. And he was the one who 'taught them as one who had authority and not as the scribes', the one to whom 'all authority in heaven and on earth' had been committed (Mark 1:22; Matt. 28:18). It was the Christ, the Son of Man, the Son of God, who took upon him the form of the Servant. He had irrefragable credentials had he wished to rely on status and authority. But he resolutely refused to countenance any such suggestion. To him the authority of the servant lay simply in the fact of his service. The divine call, the divine equipment by the Holy Spirit were demonstrated in a life of obedience, witness and endurance. These, and not some ecclesiastical counterpart to Gentile hierarchy or Jewish succession (Luke 22:25; Matt. 23:7,8), were to be the authenticating marks of Christian ministry.

When we reflect on the history of the church, are we not bound to confess that she has all too often failed to follow the model set by her founder? Frequently she has worn the robes of the ruler, not the towel of the servant. Even in our own day it can hardly be said that the brand image of the church is a society united in love for Jesus and devoted to selfless service of others.

If the whole church has failed, the ministry has failed even more signally to exhibit the character of the Servant. Even when we leave the past out of account, where pope and pastor, bishop and minister, priest and synod have all alike at times domineered over those in their charge instead of being examples to the flock (1 Pet. 5:3), the present is nothing to be proud about. Do vicars give the impression of being the servant of their people? Do they not rather behave, as too often the missionary has behaved, like little tin gods, loving to be recognised and looked up to, anxious that nothing shall go on in the parish without their personal supervision? Is it not an astonishing reversal of the pattern left by Jesus when a bishop, a chief pastor in the flock, revels in the title 'My Lord'? The whole gamut of ecclesiastical titles, from 'Father' to 'Reverend', from 'Venerable' to 'Very Reverend' give quite the wrong impression and distance their holders from the people they are called to serve.

Even today in the ecumenical scene, does the ministry seek to commend itself by the marks of the Servant, or are not the issues quite differently drawn up? When Rome insists on submission to the Roman pontiff as 'altogether necessary to salvation for every human creature' (the Bull *Unam Sanctam*) is this the way of Jesus?

The question is vital and urgent. It is a nettle that must be grasped. In today's world there is an increasing unwillingness to accept tradition or authoritarian pronouncements from any source on doctrine or ethics. In the ecumenical field, greater rapprochement is threatened by heavily entrenched doctrines of ministry which are quite uninfluenced by the example and teaching of Jesus. And in most parts of the developing world there is a continuing desire for help from the older churches, provided that such new-style missionaries come like their master 'not to be served, but to serve'. Unless more than lip service is paid to this pattern of the Servant in ministry, the prospects of advance in any of these three fields remain lamentably small.

3

A CHURCHFUL OF MINISTERS

Did the early church follow up the ideals of service laid down by Jesus? Or were they overwhelmed by the patterns of leadership all round them in pagan society?

Ministry for all Christians

The New Testament gives no suggestion that one could possibly be a Christian without at the same time being called to some ministry within the church. The Christian is indeed 'saved to serve'. St. Paul, for one, could never forget that the voice of the ascended Christ at his conversion had said: 'Rise and stand upon your feet; for I have appeared to you for this purpose, to appoint you *to serve and bear witness*' (Acts 26:16). It is hardly surprising, therefore, that the whole point of his argument in Romans 12 and 1 Corinthians 12 is that every member of the church has his or her part to play in the service of God. All without exception have a ministry.

Three words in particular are used to describe the devoted service of people who know themselves to have been forgiven.

1. The first is *doulos*. It means, quite baldly, bondslave. And it comes a great many times in the New Testament. It was a word which Paul sometimes used to describe his relation to his converts (1 Cor. 9:19; 2 Cor. 4:5) but more often his relation to Jesus. He was 'the bondslave of Jesus Christ' (Rom. 1:1, etc.). He spoke of wearing the chain of the slave, of being branded with the marks of the slave (2 Tim. 1:16; Gal. 6:17). He saw wholehearted dedication to Jesus as the only possible reaction of the redeemed. 'You are not your own; you were bought with a price,' he asserts (1 Cor. 6:19, 20). Peter makes the same plea on the same grounds: 'You know that you were ransomed ... with the precious blood of Christ' (1 Pet. 1:18, 19), and he describes apostate Christians as 'denying the master who bought them' (2 Pet. 2:1).

This metaphor of the slave was particularly telling in the first century. Roman slaves belonged entirely to their masters. They had no rights in law, and could demand no privileges. Their money, their time, their future, their marriage were all, strictly speaking, at the disposal of their masters. That is what it meant to be slaves. And that is the image that the New Testament writers deliberately took over.

But it was not applied only to the apostles or the leadership. To be sure, they are included; and Paul and Peter, James and Jude delight to call themselves the bondslaves of Jesus (Jas. 1:1; Jude 1). But it is a characteristic description of all Christians without distinction (Rev. 1:1; 1 Pet. 2:16). Could anything show more graphically their loving devotion and total dedication to Christ? Should this not shame into silence our arguments about the status and validity of ministers? The highest ministry of all is open to all – to be bondslaves of Jesus Christ.

2. The second word used of Christian service is *leitourgos*, from which we get our word 'liturgy'. If *doulos* speaks particularly of Christian devotion to Christ, *leitourgos* speaks of Christian worship of God. This is the word used of angels in heaven and men on earth when they worship the Lord and surrender themselves in loving adoration to him (Heb. 1:14; Luke 1:23; Acts 13:2).

Sometimes the Jewish background of the term is uppermost, as in the Epistle to the Hebrews, where it is made very clear that the Old Testament priestly offerings, though ineffectual in themselves, are filled with meaning when seen in the light of Christ's work (Heb. 8:2; 10:11,12).

On the other hand, Paul draws on the imagery of pagan worship when he calls the faith of the Philippians a 'liturgy' (Phil. 2:17). Christian giving is described in this way (2 Cor. 9:12; Rom. 15:27). It is the practical outworking of genuine worship of God. And for Epaphras to give himself, for the Lord's sake, to the service of Paul was no less worthy of the name (Phil. 2:30). When Paul preaches the gospel to the heathen, this too is *leitourgia* (Rom. 15:16) because through it the converts are 'offered' to God. In short, this word speaks of the service of God in worship and work. It is brought before us as the right and duty of every Christian (even, in Romans 13:6, of a pagan magistrate exercising his responsibilities dutifully). In no way is it something which is restricted or delegated to any one class within the church.

3. The third and most common word to describe a minister is *diakonos*, from which our word 'deacon' is derived. It is, like the other two, applied to all and sundry within the church. Jesus and the apostles are

called by this name: so are the humblest believers. It refers particularly to service of others, often menial service at that. The varieties of such service are vast. In Acts 6, for instance, the apostles were ministering the word of God to the people and the seven were administering famine relief. Both are styled *diakonia* (Acts 6:1–4). The New Testament does not follow our false distinction between the sacred and the secular. The whole of life is hallowed by God's creation, Christ's incarnation, and our conscious offering of all we do to him. The early church was well aware that it was called to carry on the work of the Servant.

We find the word *diakonia* used in 1 Corinthians 16:15 of what we would call church work. It is no less appropriate to the personal service rendered by Timothy and Erastus to Paul (Acts 19:22) – including, no doubt, taking down his letters, washing his clothes and cooking his meals. Prison visiting is given this honourable title in Philemon 13, and so is evangelistic preaching in Acts 20:24. Indeed, glancing through the Acts alone, you see the breadth of this term. It is applied to the ministry of feeding hungry people (Acts 6:1); the ministry of teaching hungry minds (Acts 6:4); the ministry of prayer (Acts 6:4); the ministry of giving to Christians in need in another country (Acts 11:29); the ministry of evangelism (Acts 21:19); the ministry of humble assistance as and when required (Acts 19:22); the ministry of living the whole of life for Christ even in the face of suffering and hardship (Acts 20:24). *Diakonia*, in short, belonged to the whole church and to every member of it. No service was regarded as too menial or exacting if it would commend the gospel of the grace of God.

Emil Brunner[1] put it succinctly:

One thing is supremely important; that *all* minister, and that nowhere is to be perceived a separation, or even merely a distinction, between those who do and those who do not minister, between the active and the passive members of the body, between those who give and those who receive. There exists in the *Ecclesia* a universal duty and right of service, a universal readiness to serve, and at the same time the greatest possible differentiation of functions.

Specialised ministries for some Christians

The fact that service is the hallmark of all Christians does not dispense with the need for specialisation within the Christian community. St. Paul sees the church as the Body of Christ, that is to say the agent of his purposes and bearer of his life in the world. Christians are like members within the human body; they have different functions, offer different types of service to the whole body, and are alike under the unified direction of the head.

Romans 12:4–8 urges Christians to discover and make the most of their God-given abilities for the good of the whole. Paul mentions the *charismata* (love-gifts from God) of prophecy, helpful service, teaching, encouragement, giving, leadership and pastoral concern as examples of what he means; and love is the bond which unites these diverse gifts into the harmonious unity of the Body. The function of leadership within the church is just one of the many gifts of God to his people.

1 Corinthians 12 uses the same metaphor, and makes the added point that this differentiation of function within the Body is a sovereign act of God the holy Trinity (v. 4–6). The church is seen as a living organism in which God gives different

tasks for each member to embody. Indeed, the contributions of various parts of the whole are described in this passage by four interesting words. They are *pneumatica*, functions assigned by the Holy Spirit. They are *charismata*, gracious enduements by God for service. They are *energemata*, a word which suggests the power in which these gifts are to be exercised. They are *diakoniai*, different types of service to and in the Body. Paul concludes the chapter by applying all this to a variety of ministries within the Corinthian church. They fall roughly into four groupings: ministry of the word ('first apostles, second prophets, third teachers'); ministry of healing ('then workers of miracles, then healers'); ministry of leadership and administration ('helpers, helmsmen' – what a superbly illuminating title for Christian leadership!); and finally the ministry the Corinthians (wrongly) prized the most, 'speakers in various kinds of tongues' and their interpretation. God's purpose is that by mutual caring members should use their gifts for the good of the whole Body.

Ephesians 4:8–13 underlines this theme. Paul is speaking of the gifts of the ascended Christ to his church: 'and his gifts were that some should be apostles, some prophets, some evangelists, some pastors and teachers, for the equipment of the saints for the work of ministry, for building up the body of Christ'. That is a lovely description of the leaders of a church. They do not lord it over the congregation. They are not hired and fired at the whim of the congregation. They are a team. They are the farewell gift of the ascended Christ to that congregation, and their special task is to build up the members for their work of service.

It can hardly be accidental that each of the ministries mentioned here is a ministry of the word. They exist within the Body to equip the church to play its part in the world.

In his book *Let My People Grow*[2] Michael Harper has given considerable care to studying these five ministries of apostle, prophet, evangelist, shepherd and teacher. He argues most convincingly that all five represent facets of ministry in any healthy church.

We need the apostolic deposit in scripture and the circulating, supervising role which is now embodied in bishops and travelling teachers.

Equally we need the prophetic ministry. It belonged to the foundation layer of the church (Eph. 2:20; 3:5) and it has not died out. God still guides his people through prophecy, that is, a word from himself directly applicable to the situation of that church. As early as the *Didache* at the end of the first century it was necessary to test prophecy carefully: credulity is no Christian virtue. Thus 'No prophet who orders a meal while "in the Spirit" shall eat of it; otherwise he is a false prophet.' (11.7) Very shrewd advice! But none the less the *Didache* has the highest respect for the genuine prophet. Abuse does not abolish use, and one of the crying needs in the contemporary church is the recovery of the prophetic gift.

Every church needs evangelists. These may or may not be ordained people. It is the gift that is needed, not the ordination! A church that does not evangelise will slowly die. And if it has nobody in it with an evangelistic gift, that aspect of its ministry to the world around is likely to atrophy. All Christians are called to witness to Christ. But some Christians have a special gift of evangelism, and this gift is to be valued and used in the congregation.

Pastors are no less vital. People need caring for. Troubles need to be spilled out and problems shared.

In every congregation there are those who have gifts in this direction. They constitute a priceless part of the leadership of the church, an invaluable gift from the ascended Christ for the benefit of his Body.

Finally, teachers are indispensable. Probably these are the same as the 'teachers' of 1 Corinthians 12:28 and the presbyter-bishops of Acts 20 and the Pastoral Epistles: in both places great emphasis is placed on their teaching the word of God (Acts 20:24–32; 1 Tim. 3:2; Titus 1:9). This teaching function, we are told (Eph. 4:11,12) is the supreme task of what we would call the ordained ministry, that is the part of the Body expressly charged with the duty of equipping the 'saints' for their service in the world.

Now surely this is a very remarkable thing. We tend to assume today that the purpose of the clergy is primarily to do with leading public worship and celebrating the sacraments. These functions are never once attributed to the ordained ministry in the New Testament! The ministry there is first and foremost concerned with *didache*, the teaching of Christians so that they may more effectively be the church in the world. That is to say, ministry exists for the sake of the church (and not vice versa, as is so often either taught or implied), just as the church in her turn exists for the sake of the world. The pattern of the Servant remains.

Clergy and laity?

One of the most firmly held assumptions in any of the mainline churches is that there is a clear distinction between clergy or ministers and lay people. Christianity is like a train with two classes of passenger in it. The clergy are the first-class passengers in this particular train. They are the professionals, and the lay people the amateurs; they are the priests, and the rest are the people.

All this would have sounded very strange to New Testament ears. They knew nothing of any such distinction! And this is all the more amazing when you recall that every society in the world, including Israel, had its specialised holy seasons, holy places and holy people. In Christianity all three were abolished – or rather universalised. The keeping of holy days was a matter of indifference to the early Christians (Rom. 14:5,6). They had no holy buildings, but met in private houses (e.g. Rom. 16:23): the incarnation had made the secular sacred. As to holy people, why, all believers were called to be that holy people, that universal priesthood envisaged long ago in the Old Testament but never hitherto realised (1 Pet. 2:5). The mediation of Jesus had abolished the need for an intermediary caste of priests. All can have access to God by virtue of his sacrifice. All are charged with the priestly responsibility of interceding for people before God. There is no priestly body within Christianity. It is a one-class society, though you would never guess as much, so grossly has conformity to pagan and Old Testament models distorted this unique facet of Christ's community. Although not all people are called to the function of Christian leadership, the church remains a one-class society. There is no suggestion to be found within the New Testament of what subsequently developed into the disastrous two-class system of clergy and laity.

The etymology of the two words is interesting and their usage suggestive. Clergy derives from *kleros*, God's lot or heritage. Laity comes from *laos*, the people of God. These words are not contrasted in the New Testament. *All* Christians constitute God's *kleros* (Acts 26:18; Col. 1:12 and supremely 1 Pet. 5:3

where the word is used of what we would call the laity!). *All* Christians, equally, go to make up God's *laos* (2 Cor. 6:16; 1 Pet. 2:9,10). Just as the distinction between those who do and those who do not minister is abolished in Christ, so is the age-old divide between the professional and the amateur, the cleric and the lay person. The church belongs to the new age, the age of the kingdom of God, in which distinctions of status are done away with. So in the New Testament you do not find two standards of behaviour, one for the specially holy professional people and one for the ordinary Christians. The New Testament knows nothing of a priestly caste within the church. As J.B. Lightfoot put it in his celebrated *Essay on The Christian Ministry* 'the Christian ideal is a holy season extending the whole year round, a temple confined only by the limits of the habitable world, and a priesthood coextensive with the human race.'[3] Of course, the early Christians did not for that reason forgo efficiency and organisation. To be sure, certain people generally led the services, which normally took place in this or that house. But this did not compromise the principle of the one-class society. Hear Lightfoot again:

> For communicating instruction and for preserving public order, for conducting public worship and dispensing social charities, it became necessary to appoint special officers. They are called stewards of God, servants or ministers of the church, and the like; but the sacerdotal title is never once conferred upon them. The only priests under the gospel, designated as such in the New Testament, are the saints, the members of the Christian brotherhood (1 Pet. 2:5,9; Rev. 1:6; 5:10; 20:6)[4]

That is why there is no hard and fast distinction between clergy and laity in the New Testament. All alike are the servants and ministers of God. The New Testament offers us a churchful of ministers!

When the first edition of this book emerged, back in the 1960s, entitled *Called to Serve*, there was very little on the market that spoke enthusiastically about the ministry which all Christians are called to offer. Mercifully, in recent years a tremendous change has taken place. Lay training institutes abound. Places like Regent College, Vancouver, and Christian Impact in London are proliferating. And their main aim is to equip lay Christians for the ministry that is rightly theirs, but to which the church has been blinded for so long. The Roman Catholic Church is enthusing about the 'lay apostolate' and important books about lay ministry and lay training are being written. This is a most encouraging development. But we have a very long way to go before the average Christian in the average church recognises that he or she is called by Christ to be one of his ministers.

4

FAREWELL GIFT

One has only to voice the sentiments conveyed in the last chapter to be accused of having a low view of the ordained ministry. Actually, nothing could be further from the truth. If we take seriously the teaching we have just examined in Ephesians 4:7–16, we are driven to a very high doctrine of the ordained ministry.

But let us first of all exclude two contrasting errors which prevent us having a balanced perception of what the ordained ministry is and what it is meant to achieve. We need to avoid the twin but opposite errors of clericalism and anti-clericalism, of prelacy and anarchy, which equally stand condemned in the light of the New Testament.

Two contrasting errors

There is a tendency in some circles, and by no means only 'Catholic' ones, for the ordained ministers to lord it over the flocks committed to them. Nothing of any importance in the church can be done if they are not there. The wishes of the people in matters as widely different as ritual or policy are subordinated to their own. I have known parishes where the parochial council or vestry does not even exercise its statutory say in the finances of the church; they are administered entirely by the rector. I know of others where the parish priests do not even allow meetings for Bible reading and prayer to take place in private homes unless they are present. These are extreme, but by no means isolated examples of the danger of overvaluing the office of the ordained person. It is bad for the clergy in such a situation; bad too for the congregation. It gives the former an exaggerated view of their own importance in the Body, and hinders the initiative and ministries of the latter. Wherever the principle of Romans 12, of diversity in unity, is forgotten, the church suffers. When one member exceeds his or her place, the whole Body is impoverished.

Equally dangerous, and scarcely less widespread, is a tendency to disparage the ordained ministry. This has, of course, sprung up as a reaction against long years of clerical domination. Some Christians, notably the Brethren, have no ordained ministry at all. Others interpret the priesthood of all believers as though it meant the priesthood of no believers. Others, as B.L. Manning once warned the Congregationalists, fall into the mistake of regarding the sacred ministry as a 'secretaryship, a sort of general manager's job, a device to save trouble for the majority of the church members by concentrating nearly all their duties upon one or two.'[1] This is to forget that ministers are not merely the servants of the church but the servants of Christ. It is from Christ that they derive their authority, and it is to Christ that they owe their allegiance. During his earthly life Jesus took great pains to train those whom he later commissioned as his apostles. After his resurrection he continued to 'give' ministers to his people (Eph. 4:11). There are those who 'bear rule' in the Christian churches (Heb. 13:7; 1 Thess. 5:12; 1 Tim. 5:17) and consequently there are those who are ruled. The church is not a democracy.

The ordained ministry combines both the dignity and the lowliness of Jesus who commissions it.

For the truth lies neither with clericalism nor anti-clericalism. The key to a right understanding is to realise that the ordained ministry is a parting gift of the ascended Christ. 'When he ascended on high he led a host of captives and he gave gifts to men.' What were these gifts? No less than the ordained ministry! 'His gifts were that some should be apostles, some prophets, some evangelists, some pastors and teachers, for the equipment of the saints for the work of ministry, for building up the Body of Christ.' (Eph. 4:8,11,12). Had you ever thought of local ministers as God's gift to the church? That is what they are meant to be. Then you will neither undervalue them as if they were nothing, nor overvalue them as if nothing could happen without them. Ministers are a gift to the Body.

And what are they for? This is a topic of widespread uncertainty these days. No longer are the clergy the best-educated members of society. No longer are they the main teaching influence or caring agency. They are not even any longer community leaders. Then what are they for? For taking services or validating sacraments, or burying, baptising and marrying? No. They are for building up the saints for their work of service. They are, as it were, petrol-pump attendants to get other cars mobile. They are enablers of other men and women. That is what they are for.

And the minister does not stand alone. We have already seen in Chapter One that the ministry in early days was a shared one. We shall have occasion to look further into that, since the exposure, the loneliness and the autocracy of the sole minister is a great factor in the current disenchantment with the church. This very passage specifies no less than five types of ministry which are designated as Christ's gift to the church: not one type – let alone one person in whom all the gifts are supposed to be combined by the wave of a hand at ordination! No, ministry should always be shared. That complementarity in unity is one of the aspects of God himself which he intends to see reproduced in the leadership of his people. Solitude in ministry is no more God's plan than solitude in home or family life. The gift of God is not a ministerial figurehead, but a partnership of ministry.

So the leadership in a church is called to be neither complaisant nor authoritarian. They must be first and foremost servants of the Lord and then of the people they are called to serve; dedicated to the task of bringing them to Christian maturity, anxious to ensure that every part of the Body is working properly, so that the whole Body can be effective in representing Christ to a sceptical world. Only in such an extension of the work of the Servant can the true balance between the authority and the lowliness of the ordained ministry be preserved.

What is ordination?

We have been speaking all this time about the ordained ministry as if everyone knew what it was. Instead, it is a matter for sharp debate. It is clear from the New Testament that leaders were identifiable and diverse. We have already seen five types of leadership mentioned in Ephesians. If we look in New Testament ordination for a specific setting aside of three orders of ministry, bishops, priests and deacons, we shall look in vain. But if we ask whether the leadership, diverse as it undoubtedly was, was set aside specifically for the task with prayer, fasting and the imposition of hands, we shall find that this was the case.

In Acts 14:23 we read that Paul and Barnabas appointed 'elders' or 'presbyters' (it is the same word in Greek) in every church they had brought into being during the first missionary journey. The word used is *cheirotoneo*, which in later ecclesiastical usage means to impose hands in ordination. However, in secular usage the word simply means to 'choose' or 'appoint' (in Greek city-states the people originally exercised their choice by raising their hands). Such is the meaning of the word in its only other appearance in the New Testament (2 Cor. 8:19), and in its three occurrences in Ignatius (*Philad.* 10.1; *Smyrn.* 11.2; *Poly.* 7.2), so you cannot be absolutely sure that Paul and Barnabas laid hands on these people to ordain them. In Acts 6 it is uncertain whether the apostles or the people lay hands on the seven; in any case it is not clear whether this is an ordination or an *ad hoc* measure to relieve a particular situation. The only other evidence from the New Testament concerns Timothy. Paul speaks of 'the gift of God which is within you through the laying on of my hands' (2 Tim. 1:6). This may refer to Timothy's ordination. It may equally indicate his baptism which was in those days accompanied by the laying on of hands (Heb. 6:1,2; Acts 9:17). If so, the only certain reference to ordination in the New Testament would be 1 Timothy 4:14. This may be translated with the R.S.V., 'Do not neglect the gift you have, which was given you by prophetic utterance when the elders laid their hands upon you.' Or it may mean, as Daube[2] and Jeremias[3] have suggested 'when hands were laid upon you with the object of making you a presbyter.' Whichever is right, we see a primitive example of the solemn imposition of hands commissioning a person for ministry by those who were recognised as competent authorities in the church. These might be either an apostle (as perhaps in the case of Timothy) or an apostolic delegate (see Titus 1:5 and 1 Tim. 5:22) or those who were already elders (1 Tim. 4:14). There would thus be a public recognition by the Body of Christ of the gift of leadership imparted by God to a particular member; and a commissioning of that person, through their representatives, to exercise that gift for the benefit of the Body as a whole. In that sense, and in that sense alone, is there any difference between clergy and laity in the New Testament.

Coming to the modern church, the question 'What is ordination?' can be answered at two levels.

At the organisational level the answer in most churches is unambiguously clear. It is seen in terms of status and authorisation. In the Anglican Church, to which I belong, it is the authorisation by the bishop to pronounce the absolution, to preach the word of God, and to administer the sacraments.

But what is ordination at a deeper and theological level? It is the 'setting apart, because of God's calling, of those who exercise a ministry of the Word logically prior to other ministries, which enables the church to develop into the pure Body of Christ.'[4] It is 'a call to the service of leadership, addressed publicly to a believer, by which the church sanctions the call of God.'[5] The essential theological point has been clearly grasped by Michael Harper[6]: 'Ordination is essentially a recognition of abilities already evidenced in the life of a person and the authorisation of that person to exercise his gifts in the body of Christ.' There need be no battle between charism and office in the church so long as ordination is the public recognition by the people of God of the charism of leadership already evidenced, at least germinally, in the candidates.

If, then, we look for a setting aside of ministers by prayer and the imposition of hands, there is clear evidence for it in the New Testament. If we construe this ministry too narrowly, we shall go wrong. Presbyter-bishops, apostolic delegates, deacons both male and female, prophets and prophetesses, evangelists, pastors and teachers all qualify as that enabling ministry through which the rest of the Body is edified. Indeed, it is encouraging to see that it is being broadened, by the far greater emphasis that is being given in recent times to lay ministries and most obviously, of course, in the Church of England, by the ordination of women.

Would it be too radical to suggest that the way in which the ministry of various members in local churches in deprived areas as well as flourishing ones, could best be furthered would be by the bishop (or other competent authority) setting apart with prayer and the laying on of hands those within the congregation who display the *charism* of leadership? This would, after all, merely be an extension of the representative idea that the whole people of God may, as a matter of order, be represented by a person authorised to act in the name of the congregation – a principle which underlies 'ordination' as we know it at present. Such people need not attend a theological college provided that they were carefully trained on the job, supervised and encouraged. They would earn their bread and butter from a secular calling, but their supreme concern would be for the building up of Christ's people. It might be proper to restrict their leadership to the local community where they live — they might not necessarily be called to the same role if they moved to another community. The important thing is that by recognising those who have the God-given charism of leadership in the church (which may well be displayed by those who are by no means natural leaders in secular life) we would be following an important New Testament principle of recognising and ordaining tried local leaders. In this way money would be saved, and the unedifying practice of churches being herded together into a Group or Team irrespective of pastoral considerations would be avoided. So would the ridiculous expedient of one 'ordained' person running around half a dozen churches administering Holy Communion, just because they have not got their own 'minister'. Some tentative experiments are currently being made in this direction: Lay Readers and locally ordained ministers are being given more responsibility in the Church. Financial circumstances are forcing changes. Such circumstances could be welcomed as an opportunity allowing the rediscovery of a New Testament pattern of local leadership and ministry.

Ordained and other ministries

It is clear that all Christians are called to serve. It is also clear from the New Testament that some Christians are charged with a ministry of the word and of leadership which is a facilitating ministry and is logically prior to other ministries within the Body of Christ. Does this mean that there should be inviolable separate spheres for 'clergy' and 'laity'? We have already looked at this in principle, and seen that there is no theological justification for it. But let us look now at three areas normally restricted to the 'clergy' and see how the principle might work out in practice.

1. *Teaching the faith* is an important function of the specialised ministry. And yet in the Corinthian church there was room for any member to take part in the ministry of the word if he or she had something to contribute (1 Cor. 14:26–29). Indeed, the fact that any member of the congregation may speak out for the Lord is what powerfully convinces the unbeliever

coming in that God is in their midst (1 Cor. 14:24, 25). Clearly, then, while teaching is the special function of what we might call the 'ordained ministry' it is not exclusively theirs. I see no reason why men and women in our congregations should not teach the faith in the collegiality of leadership which goes to make up a healthy church.

2. *Leading in worship* may well have been a function of the 'ordained ministry' (though we are not expressly told so); but there is no indication that it should be restricted to them. On the contrary, any member of the congregation was free to contribute teaching, a prophetic utterance or picture, a hymn or psalm, even a contribution in tongues, provided it was interpreted, so that the Body could be edified (1 Cor. 14:26ff). For centuries the element of *risk* in vital corporate worship of this kind has seemed too great: there is very little danger of disorder arising from excessive congregational participation in the older established churches of the world!

In some of the younger churches that risk is being taken, and is being justified. The growth of Pentecostal churches (and charismatic congregations within the older denominations) is one of the undeniable features in the religious life of our day. This growth may be due to many causes, but high among them must feature the large extent of lay participation. Every Christian among them sees it as a duty and privilege to take part in the leading of worship as and when appropriate, and to bear witness to Christ at home, at work or in the open air when that is called for. The saints have been equipped, in however inadequate a way, for service; and they grow in spiritual effectiveness, joy and commitment because they are actually involved rather than being, as in many a church, almost an audience of spectators. There can be no justification for restricting the leadership in worship to the clergy exclusively.

3. A third area which, above all, has been associated with the clergy alone is *the celebration of the sacraments*. It is significant that in the New Testament we are never told who should baptise and who should preside at the Communion. It apparently never occurred to the first generation of Christians that these actions hung together as a specific area into which no 'lay' person might trespass. The word 'sacrament' is never found in the New Testament. It is derived from the heathen world of the Graeco-Roman society, and although it is none the worse for that, it seems to have brought pagan ideas over with it. There is a good deal of truth in Emil Brunner's contention[7] that with Ignatius's emphasis early in the second century on the Eucharist as the *pharmakon athanasias* 'the medicine of immortality' and the bishop as the only distributor of it (*Ephes*. 20:2) we have passed from the New Testament conception of the church as a unity of persons redeemed by Christ and united in the Spirit, to an idea of the church as a collective whose unity flows from their common relationship to a thing, the sacrament. Be that as it may, it seems reasonably clear that in the New Testament anyone can baptise. As Eduard Schweizer put it[8]: 'The apostles do not as a rule baptise (Acts 10:48, cf. 19:5 beside 6a, 1 Cor. 1:14–17). Ordinary church members do (Acts 9:18).' An overstatement no doubt, but the point is made!

It seems likely, too, that any suitably respected leader could preside at the Lord's Supper in the early days of the church. When Paul had to rebuke abuses in the church at Corinth there is no one individual he can blame. And if in Acts 2:46 the 'breaking of bread from house to house' refers to the Eucharist, as it probably does, then that settles the matter. It is expressly stated that this is what the *converts* did. It was a lay celebration. In the Pastoral Epistles Paul expresses great concern over church order, but he never suggests that the celebration of the Eucharist or baptism is a function peculiar either to the presbyter-bishops whom Timothy and Titus are to ordain, or to the apostolic delegates themselves. Even as late as Justin in the middle of the second century (1 *Apology*, 65) we find the celebrant simply referred to as *ho prohestōs* 'the president', presumably because, as in the *Didache*, it is not yet invariably the task of one particular official.

I am not in the least advocating ecclesiastical anarchy. I am just seeking to separate principle from long-established custom. The principle is that Christianity knows of no special priestly cadre within Christ's priestly Body, the church. All Christians, not some, are called to minister. And this ministry will be as diverse as that of the various limbs in a human body. It is perfectly right and proper that certain people should normally carry out certain functions. What is wrong is to insist that nobody else can possibly carry them out even in an emergency. Thus in England there is normally no reason why 'lay' people should celebrate the Communion: there are enough ordained people to do so, at least in most parts of the land. But this is not the case in many missionary situations. On average eight women offer as missionaries to every one man. They frequently act as pioneers in the evangelisation of primitive tribes in places like New Guinea and Colombia. They administer the first baptisms and Communions, handing over to the local believers as soon as possible. Are we to stay in the comfort of our Western ivory towers and proclaim such ministries invalid? We may do so if we wish. But we shall find no warrant in the New Testament for our position. There we are not presented with a hierarchy of ministers but a body of co-operating members, exercising their God-given gifts and functions for the good of the whole, as they carry out the work of the Servant in the world. All ministry is an act of God himself, and an essential part of ministry in the New Testament is that *an unqualified person* is called to it, in order 'to show that the transcendent power belongs to God and not to us' (2 Cor. 4:7).

Soon after New Testament days, however, a development set in which changed the Christian organism with its dynamic ministries into an organisation with institutionalised officers. When Paul wrote to the Corinthians he urged them to submit to their leaders in recognition of the quality of their service (1 Cor. 16:15,16). When Clement of Rome wrote to the Corinthians, less than half a century later, he urged them to reinstate their deposed presbyters because they had been properly appointed (1 *Clement* 44). The Christian fellowship had begun to give way to the ecclesiastical institution. The dynamic view of ministry had begun to give way to the static view of 'office'. The servant had begun to savour of the master. This is a process which we in our day should seek to reverse.

5

THREEFOLD MINISTRY?

The Preface to the Anglican Ordinal asserts roundly, 'It is evident unto all men diligently reading the Holy Scriptures and Ancient Authors that from the Apostles' time there have been these Orders of Ministers in Christ's Church: Bishops, Priests and Deacons.' This statement is widely misquoted. It does not say 'there have been *three* Orders' that is, three only. It is not in the least polemical. The Reformers who framed the statement did not wish to unchurch their colleagues on the continent who had a different, perhaps presbyterian form of church government.

The views of the Reformers are well known. They agreed that all necessary doctrine was set forth in Holy Scripture: and the importance of episcopal ordination was not plainly set forth there. Thus Cranmer could say, 'I do not set more by any title, name or style than I do by the paring of an apple, further than that it shall be to the setting forth of God's word and will,'[1] and Bishop Hooper could write, 'I believe the church is bound to no sort of ministers or any ordinary succession of bishops . . . but only unto the Word of God'[2]. Article XIX sets out the marks of the church: it does not indicate that any particular form of church government is necessary. It gives, on the contrary, precisely the same marks of the visible church as are laid down in the Reformed Continental Confessions of Saxony, Augsburg and Switzerland.

What the Preface was concerned to maintain is that the Church of England, in retaining at the Reformation the catholic orders of bishop, priest and deacon, did so because they saw those orders to be agreeable both to history and to scripture. It was a principle with Cranmer in his reforming work in England to retain what of 'the old may be well used'. His judgment cannot be faulted on biblical or historical grounds. You do not only find these three titles in scripture; you also find there a threefold division of ministry – the supervisory and circulating ministry, the local and settled ministry and the assistant ministry of the deacons.

If we look at the matter historically the same conclusion is reached. Nowhere do we find a 'parity of ministers'. Everywhere we encounter gradations of offices in the church. The threefold ministry was an established fact in the Asiatic churches at the end of the apostolic period as the writings of Polycarp and Ignatius make plain. By the middle of the second century the threefold ministry of bishop, priest and deacon was the normal, almost universal pattern for Christian ministry the world over.

On the other hand, we must remember that other orders of ministry continued. Apostles, in the sense of wandering Christian leaders with a charismatic flavour, are highly regarded in the *Didache* and Ignatius. There were still prophets and prophetesses, still exorcists and miraculous healers. Witnesses as far apart as Justin in Rome (*Dial.* 38,82), Irenaeus in Gaul (*A.H.* 2.32.4,5), and Tertullian in North Africa (*de Anima* 9) not only attest their presence but regard them as part of God's ministerial gift to his church. In the Roman Church of the mid third century we find a fascinating catalogue of ministries: 46 presbyters, 7 deacons, 7 sub-deacons, 42 acolytes, and 52 exorcists, doorkeepers and readers (Eusebius *H.E.* 6.43). As a matter of fact Rome has showed more flexibility on varieties in ministry than many other churches. Jerome and Aquinas, for example, both refused to regard bishops as a different order from priests, and the Council of Trent defined that the two differed in *gradus* but not in *ordo*. It would be precarious, therefore, to interpret the Anglican Ordinal in any exclusive sense. This can easily be proved, if proof were needed, by the fact that in the sixteenth and seventeenth centuries the Church of England enjoyed the closest of ties (including intercommunion and occasional interchange of ministers), with her sister churches of the Reformation on the continent who had not retained the threefold ministry. What we may maintain with confidence is that the threefold ministry is securely grounded in both scripture and history; and so, without prejudice to other ministries, we shall proceed to examine those of bishop, priest and deacon.

Priest or presbyter

Their derivation

As we shall see later on, the Christian priest has nothing to do with the sacrificing priesthood of the Old Testament. The word is derived both historically and linguistically from the 'presbyter' or 'elder' of the New Testament.

But where did the idea come from? The answer is the Jewish synagogue. Any ten Jews could band together to form a synagogue, so it is hardly surprising that in Jewish areas 'Christian congregations were long called synagogues' (Jas. 2:2). The civil and administrative duties of the synagogue devolved upon a board of presbyters, who saw that the law was observed, administered taxes, and, if necessary, enforced excommunication. They had no liturgical functions: these lay in the hands of the 'ruler of the synagogue'. He was not a priest of the Aaronic line, but, like the presbyters, he was a layman elected for the office.

Such was the model conveniently to hand for the new movement. The Christians took it over and adapted it. We find Christian presbyters all over the Mediterranean basin (Acts 20:17; 14:23; 1 Pet. 5:1; cf. 1:1; Jas. 5:14). We even find them figuring prominently in John's vision of heaven, where the four and twenty elders, representing Old and New Covenants, worship God continually (Rev. 4:4).

If this is so, why do we find no mention of presbyters in Paul's letters apart from the Pastoral Epistles? Chance may have something to do with it: we would have no mention of bishops either if Philippians had not been preserved. But it seems probable that the *presbyters* (or elders) were called *bishops* (or overseers) in Gentile churches, for that word was commonly used to denote any sort of supervision in the Graeco-Roman world. Thus at Philippi, in Asia Minor, and in Crete the presbyter is styled 'bishop' (Phil. 1:1; Acts 20:28; 1 Pet. 5:2; Titus 1:7). As we shall see, the two offices were the same, and it was merely a difference of nomenclature, and it was never uniform: 'bishop' never entirely eclipsed 'presbyter' even among Gentile congregations (1 Tim. 5:17; 1 Clem. 21.44).

Furthermore there was a broad variety of expression in the New Testament and particularly among the Pauline circle, to denote the ministerial office. The function is so much more important than the name. We are probably right in identifying the 'leader' of Hebrews 13:7,17, and the 'man who bears rule' (1 Thess. 5:12,13) with the presbyter. And the 'helps and leadership' of Cor. 12:28 are two divine gifts which soon crystallised into the diaconate and presbyterate respectively.

Their work

The most interesting of these names is 'those who bear rule'. The *proistamenos* (and its cognate form, *prostates*) originally denoted the powerful Roman 'patron' who had his 'clients'. The word then came to be applied to any person of wealth and influence who used his position to benefit the less fortunate. Clement of Rome once called Jesus 'the patron of our weakness' (36.1). The word sheds a fine light on the nature of Christian leadership. It is no doubt because of her championing the cause of her poorer and less influential Christian friends that Phoebe, the deaconess of the church of Cenchreae, is given this lovely title (Rom. 16:2).

These varied titles give some idea of the tasks of ordained ministers. They are, first and foremost, *presbyters*. The word means primarily a senior person, an elder. In some of the New Testament references (e.g. 1 Tim. 5:1–3,17; 1 Pet. 5:1–5) it is notoriously hard to know whether age or office is meant. Clearly young people were not ordained: and one was generally considered a young man in both Greek and Hebrew culture until the age of forty.

Then the title *bishop* describes the main function of these elders. They are to supervise and oversee the congregations committed to them (Acts 20:28; 1 Pet. 5:2). Presbyters, or senior people is what they *are*: bishoping or oversight is what they *do*. This oversight will mean that they are *pastors* to the congregation and are also *leaders* in the church, not least, no doubt, in public worship. They are to act like *patron* to client: this will involve material assistance for the needy, and admonition of the unruly (1 Thess. 5:12) along with support for the weak (Acts 20:35). Theirs is supremely a *teaching* office, and this grew more important as the church spread and the apostles died off.

Thus their work is in some ways parallel to and in some ways much wider than that of the Jewish elder. Both bear rule, both administer, both excommunicate (this is hinted at in 1 Cor. 5:4,5). But unlike the Jewish elder the Christian minister has a pastoral and probably a liturgical function as well. Unlike them the minister is a teacher, and is entrusted with a special ministry of prayer (Jas. 5:14). Perhaps the biggest difference was this: all Christian rule was marked with the imprint of Jesus the Servant. He had both told them and shown them that the leader (*hegoumenos*) among them was to adopt the role of the servant (*diakonos*). How could they ever forget, when they used this title *hegoumenos* of Christian presbyters, that its supremacy was one of service? How could they ever be domineering over the flock in their work as bishops, so long as they kept before their eyes the oversight of Jesus, the bishop of their souls? (1 Pet. 5:3, 2:25).

A corporate and settled ministry

Two other points of some significance emerge from the rather sparse evidence of the New Testament on presbyters. The first is that they represent a corporate and settled ministry. The second is that there are not two types of presbyter.

The presbyters were the local ministers of the church, in contrast to itinerant apostles, prophets and evangelists. This comes out particularly clearly in the Jerusalem church where, in the absence of the apostles on missionary journeys, we read simply of 'the presbyters' or 'James and the presbyters' (Acts 11:30, 21:18). And, like their Jewish prototypes, they always appear in the plural throughout all the variety of titles used to describe them. They represent a collegiality of leadership, in striking contrast to most of their successors the world over. This is one of the areas where we most need to recapture the insight of the first Christians. At first it looks as if 1 Tim. 3:2 and Titus 1:7 are exceptions to this collegiality, but in fact this is not so. Paul tells his lieutenant Titus to ordain 'presbyters in every city . . . if any be blameless . . . for a bishop must be blameless.' In other words the singular, 'the bishop' is a generalising singular; the presbyters and the bishop are one and the same here as they are in the rest of the New Testament. Presbyters point us to the need for a fellowship of leadership in the church.

The Presbyterian Churches have been better than most of the rest of us in retaining this corporate leadership. But they have often made a sharp division between 'ruling elders' and 'teaching elders', following Calvin in Book 4 of the *Institutes*. The question turns on the interpretation of 1 Tim. 5:17 'Let the elders who rule well be considered worthy of double honour (or *pay*), especially those who labour in preaching and teaching.' There can be little doubt that all elders 'rule'. It seems to be implied, though, that not all elders labour at preaching and teaching. So does this mean there is an elite within the presbyteral board which spends itself in preaching and teaching? There is no suggestion elsewhere in the New Testament that this is so: many Presbyterians no longer hold it; and J.B. Lightfoot[3] plausibly interprets the verse as meaning 'as each has his special gift, so would he devote himself more or less exclusively to the one or the other of these sacred functions.' As one who has worked in such a team of presbyters for ten years I can only say that that is how in fact it works. There is one leadership group, but members within it have different and complementary gifts: that is what makes group leadership so important and so valuable for the church.

On any showing, the presbyterate in the early church showed a far more corporate oversight than most modern churches. The virtual autocracy of many a parish priest or nonconformist minister today is good neither for them nor for the congregation; it is clearly at variance with the pattern of Christian leadership in the New Testament; and it obscures the portrait of the servant.

Bishops

Presbyter-bishops
In the New Testament bishops and presbyters or priests are the same. This, as Lightfoot showed, is the plain meaning of the texts, and his view is universally accepted nowadays.

The evidence for this identification of bishop and presbyter is as follows. In Acts 20 the elders of v.17 (*presbyteroi*) are called to exercise the function of bishops (*episkopountes*) in v.28. In 1 Peter 5:1,2 the presbyters are again, in most manuscripts, told to 'act as bishops' of the flock, though some important manuscripts omit the word *episkopountes*. If the word is not part of the original text its later inclusion is amazing, in view of the separation which was soon to come between bishop and presbyters. In 1 Timothy 3:1–7 we have a description of a bishop followed immediately by the requirements for a deacon, while in 1 Timothy 5:17–19 the former ministers are referred to and called presbyters. Titus, as we have seen, is told to 'appoint elders in every town . . . for a bishop must be blameless' (Titus 1:5–7). Jerome in his comment on this passage says bluntly *idem est ergo presbyter qui episcopus* – 'the bishop is therefore the same as the presbyter.' We can only draw the same conclusion from Philippians 1:1 with its 'bishops and deacons'. We can hardly imagine Paul singling out the first and third orders of ministry, omitting the second, and throwing in the extra anomaly of a plurality of bishops! Clement of Rome knows bishops and presbyters are identical. Like Paul in Philippians 1:1 Clement three times mentions bishops and deacons together – and the whole aim of his letter is to reinstate the deposed presbyters (Chs 42–44). In the *Didache* too, we meet just two orders, bishops and deacons. As late as the fourth century memories of this early usage survive. The *Apostolic Constitutions* (2.26–8) maintain that it is the presbyters who stand in the place of the apostles. This is not an anti-episcopal claim; it is a recognition that in New Testament times bishops and presbyters were identical.

The rise of the episcopate

How then did they get separated? Manifestly they very soon did. Ignatius, whose lifetime certainly overlapped considerably with that of St. John, shows that monepiscopacy, that is, rule by a single bishop, was a regular feature in the churches of Asia Minor in his own day. As bishop he relates to the bishops of Ephesus, Philadelphia and so forth. He is almost obsessed with the importance of the episcopate, and he often speaks with great clarity about the three-fold ministry. Thus in *Magnesians* 6 he pleads, 'Do all things in unity, under the bishop presiding in the place of God, the presbyters in the place of the council of the apostles, and the deacons . . . who are entrusted with the service of Jesus Christ.' He has nothing to say about apostolic succession, though we learn from Tertullian (*Adv. Marc.* 4.5) and Clement of Alexandria (in Eusebius *H.E.* 3.23) that the apostle John went round in his old age appointing bishops in Asia Minor. This seems very possible. How else could bishops have become so marked a feature in proconsular Asia within a decade of John's death?

No doubt the very stridency of Ignatius's claims of monepiscopacy indicates that it was not as firmly established as he would like. It may well have come to the West considerably later. The Roman church was, as we have seen, governed by a board of presbyters in Clement's day at the end of the first century, and the same held good thirty or forty years later when Hermas wrote. He twice refers to bishops, each time in the plural, and otherwise speaks of the 'elders who preside over the church' (*Vis.* 3.5.1, *Sim.* 9.27.2, *Vis.* 2.4). It is significant that whereas Ignatius could write to the bishop in the Eastern churches, he could not do so at Rome. Nor could his contemporary, Polycarp. Although himself a bishop in the Ignatian sense (Ignatius, *Polyc.* 1.1) he knows that this form of church polity does not obtain at Philippi. And so, with gracious Christian tact, he begins his letter, 'Polycarp and the presbyters with him, to the church of God sojourning at Philippi.' He makes no mention of the bishop anywhere in his letter, but refers to the Philippian leaders as 'presbyters' and 'deacons' (6.1,5.2). This was probably written in A.D. 115. It is plain that monepiscopacy was unevenly distributed in the first half of the second century. Thereafter it became universal.

The background of episcopacy

What is the background of this office that springs immediately to full flower in the pages of Ignatius? Nobody really knows. There is no obvious parallel in Judaism, though attempts have been made, unsuccessfully, to derive the Christian bishop from the *hazzan* of the synagogue or the *mebhakkér* of the Covenanters at Qumran. Several of the Fathers agree in seeing James of Jerusalem as the first bishop, or even as the 'bishop of bishops'. But James owed his position of undoubted supremacy at Jerusalem to his blood relationship with Jesus: this is underlined by the fact that when he was martyred in the early sixties 'Symeon, the son of Cleophas, our Lord's uncle, was appointed the second bishop, whom all proposed, as the cousin of the Lord' (Eusebius, *H.E.* 4.22). Clearly, we are dealing with a caliphate not an episcopate. James certainly furnished an obvious precedent for second-century bishops, with his central abode at Jerusalem, his wide supervision, and his constitutional rule along with the elders (Acts 21:18). Nevertheless by his physical connection with the Lord, and because of the destruction of his line in the early years of the second century, he actually represented the very antithesis of the emerging monepiscopacy of the Catholic Church.

If the precedents for the office are obscure, so are the stages by which it became separated from the presbyterate. However, if you have a board of elders, someone has to preside. Probably, therefore, the bishop soon emerged from the board of presbyters by virtue of his chairmanship. In the early days of the second century you find the bishop being associated with certain functions that would tend to emphasise his personal ascendancy. First, he is the man who presides at the Eucharist, where,

51

from the nature of the case, you need a single celebrant. Second, he is always in charge of the property of the church. This consisted mainly of offerings at the Communion until the church began to own buildings at the end of the second century: it would be natural, therefore, for the celebrant to handle them. Third, we find the bishop acting as the focus of unity among the various sectional interests and the house-churches of a town. 'Do nothing without the bishop. Cherish Union; shun divisions,' pleads Ignatius (*Philad.* 7). Fourth, he appears as the bastion of orthodoxy, the guardian of the apostolic faith; and this was particularly important before an authoritative canon of scripture had emerged. The succession of bishops in a see was regarded, particularly by Irenaeus, as a safeguard against heresy and a guarantee of continuity with the teachings of the apostolic age. Finally, the bishop always appears as the foreign secretary, so to speak, of the church. Through him it communicates with others, and through him hospitality is afforded to visitors from other churches. In some such ways as these, we may believe, the chairman of the board of presbyters became the bishop of Catholic Christendom.

The purpose of episcopacy

But what was the theory that lay behind monepis-copacy? I believe that quite simply the idea of sole episcopacy originated in the sole oversight of God himself. In the New Testament *episkopē* and its cognates are referred to the Holy Trinity. It is exercised by Father, Son and Spirit (Luke 19:44; 1 Pet. 2:12; 1 Pet. 2:25; Acts 20:28). *Episkopē* is, therefore, an attribute of God. In his grace, he delegates it without abdicating it. Thus all Christians are called to oversee or take care of one another (Matt. 25:36,43; Jas. 1:27; Heb. 12:15). Like servanthood and priesthood, oversight belongs to the whole church. But the church, too, concentrates that care in the hands of its ministers without its members abdicating the responsibility of caring for others. The ministers representatively take it on. No wonder Paul wrote 'If anyone aspire to *episkopē*, he desires a noble task' (1 Tim. 3:1). No wonder Ignatius exclaims that the bishop is the 'type', the representative of God, and rejoices with the Romans that after his martyrdom the church in Syria will have God for its bishop *in his place!* (*Magn.* 6.1, *Trall.* 3.1, *Rom.* 9.1). In short, *episkopē* belongs supremely to God the Holy Trinity. He shares it (without surrendering it) with the church, and with its ministers in particular. The one bishop embodies in his own person the oversight of God.

The value of episcopacy

Although therefore the Ignatian type of episcopacy cannot be found in the New Testament nor in some parts of the world for many years afterwards, nevertheless it remains true that the New Testament knows and values the pastoral oversight exercised by the apostles and their delegates over local ministers. The need for this sort of oversight did not diminish, but increased with the death of the last apostles. We need a focus of unity within the churches of a given area. We need an embodiment of the historic faith down the ages and across the globe, and this is fittingly represented in a single person. We need someone who is charged to defend the faith against attenuation or perversion; though whether the episcopate has been very successful in this respect down the centuries may be doubted. Most of all we need someone to care for the pastors of hard-pressed local churches; and nobody knows this better than the pastors themselves. On these grounds we can urge that not merely the name but the office of bishop is scriptural, primitive and of abiding value in the church.

In recent years this has become increasingly recognised among non-episcopal churches. There is value in monepiscopacy, and clearly it is the only form of church government that can possibly command universal assent in the reunion of Christendom. But that is not to say that episcopacy as traditionally exercised is ideal. The larger the diocese, the less justification there is for monepiscopacy. Sole leadership of a million or more people cannot possibly be pastoral, and runs great danger of becoming prelatical. Often counsel is darkened among advocates of episcopacy because the Ignatian arguments are applied to the present scheme of things in the West, and it is forgotten that episcopacy to Ignatius was more like a vicar's presidency over half a dozen curates than diocesan episcopacy where the bishop presides over hundreds of local churches. Ignatius does not speak to our condition, for he does not speak of our kind of bishops. If we wish to commend episcopacy we need to recover more of the sense of collegiality which Ignatius embodied. Twelve times in his letters he mentions the three orders of ministry; and in ten of them the three form an inseparable unity. Synodical government in England has gone some way towards regaining this unity, but there is still much too much decision-making in Diocesan Church House over matters which concern the parishes of the diocese, and the parishes themselves are not consulted. No wonder some Free Churchmen regard episcopacy with suspicion, even in this day and age. They feel, not without justification, that the undeniable tendency for the bishop to be transformed from an 'undershepherd' into the 'lord' of the flock is derogatory to the supreme headship of Christ over his church. The only type of episcopacy which can hope to win universal acclaim in the church of the future is one where bishops are leaders who serve their people, share decision making, and know, love and suffer with their flock.

Deacons

Our knowledge of deacons in the early church is as scanty as it is of bishops, but for a different reason. As we have seen, service, *diakonia*, was the ideal and the task of every member of the church, and there was no immediate tendency to restrict the title to any particular group within it.

The word 'deacon' is used of Jesus himself (Rom. 15:8) and Paul uses it both of Timothy's ministry and of his own (1 Tim. 4:6, 1:12). This should both remind us that all ministry in the New Testament is marked with the imprint of Jesus the Servant, and that the word is used of particular ministries only in a semi-technical sense.

An auxiliary ministry

Nevertheless, it is plain that the word was applied by the early Christians to subordinate ministries in the church: there are ministries of leadership and ministries of assistance. Deacons belong to the latter category. Leaving aside for a moment the question of whether the seven in Acts 6 were deacons in the technical sense, they are clearly an auxiliary and assistant ministry. The seven are set aside to *deacon* tables, thus releasing the apostles for their primary task of *deaconing* the word of God (Acts 6:4).

The same differentiation is to be found in 1 Cor. 12:28 in broad terms: while some are given by the Lord the task of being 'rulers' among his people, others are called to be 'helps'. To sharpen that distinction up a little, Paul speaks of 'bishops' and 'deacons' in Philippians 1:1 and 1 Timothy 3:8ff, though somewhat curiously in the very similar letter to Titus deacons are not mentioned.

The origin of the office is obscure. It seems to have been a Christian invention, otherwise Clement of Rome (ch. 42) would not have found it necessary to introduce deacons by force into the text of Isaiah 60:17! It would be nice to think that the seven of Acts 6 *were* the first deacons in the technical sense. For it would tell us that they were indeed a Christian invention; that they were ordained by prayer and the imposition of hands; that they had to be wise men full of the Holy Spirit; and that their functions beside being financial and administrative, involved preaching, apologetics and 'signs and wonders.' The later church certainly saw the seven as the first deacons, from Irenaeus onwards, so much so that the Council of Neo-Caesarea in A.D. 315 passed as one of its canons: 'The deacons ought to be seven, even if the city be great.'

Nevertheless it is a plain fact that the seven are not called 'deacons' in Acts 6; their functions of preaching and evangelism hardly correspond with the duties associated with the later diaconate; and when Philip, one of the seven, is mentioned later on in Acts he is called not 'the deacon' but 'the evangelist' (Acts 21:8). So we cannot be sure. But if the appointment of the seven is dissociated from the institution of the diaconate, we have no knowledge whatever of the origin of this office, and can only assume from Philippians 1:1 that this was the name given to a subsidiary office which assisted presbyter-bishops, particularly in financial matters. This would accord with their special mention in Philippians 1:1, for Philippians is a thank-you letter for a contribution given to Paul by the church at Philippi, of which the bishops and deacons were, no doubt, the organisers.

Their task

What were the functions of the deacons in the early church? Whether or not the seven were deacons, the task of a subsidiary ministry engaged primarily in social work and poor relief accords well enough with such scanty references to their function as we find elsewhere in the New Testament. Deacons could be male or female: Romans 16:1 tells us Phoebe was a female deacon, while Pliny, a Roman governor writing a decade into the second century, clearly refers to women deacons (*ministrae*). He tortured them in order to secure information about the Christians (Pliny, *Ep*. 10.96). 1 Timothy 3 says that deacons must be consistent in what they say, serious about their Christian life, and not greedy for money: these were important qualities in people who were constantly moving from house to house and distributing financial help. It was expected that deacons should be married and should manage their families well. 'The women' also were to be serious about their commitment, not greedy for money or wine, Christians who had proved themselves and were reliable and not given to gossip. It is not certain whether 'the women' means the women deacons or the wives of deacons – yet another tantalising gap in our knowledge. We are not told that deacons must be talented at preaching or teaching, but we are told that their lives must be exemplary, their grasp on the Christian faith comprehensive and their consciences tender.

In later generations we find the deacons closely associated with the bishop, whose assistants they became both in liturgical and in administrative functions.

This close association with the bishop not infrequently led to a deacon succeeding to the bishopric, occasionally without even being ordained priest. Two things are never forgotten about them: their embodiment of the ministry of Jesus the Servant in his church, and their supposed origin in serving tables. This was remembered both in the part they played in administering the Holy Communion, and in the task which Justin tells us fell to them afterwards, of taking the consecrated elements to any who were unable through sickness to be present at the service (1 *Apol.* 65).

In the early church a person would often remain a deacon for life, and so it is today in the Eastern Church where the deacon does a 'lay' job. However, in the West the office became a stepping-stone to the priesthood, as it still remains in the Roman and Anglican Churches. At the Reformation some attempt was made to recover the primitive diaconate, and in Congregational and Baptist Churches the 'deacon' denotes what the Presbyterian Churches prefer to call 'elder'. This is a 'lay' office and does not normally lead into the ordained ministry. Such a person is the representative of the congregation who takes part with the ordained minister in three ways in particular: assisting in administering discipline, undertaking administrative work, and distributing the elements at Holy Communion. The diaconate is awaiting rediscovery in episcopal churches, and it should become a serious subject for study and research in denominations which profess such respect for the threefold ministry. Indeed, this is already beginning to happen: with the ordination of women to the priesthood, the diaconate is no longer necessarily an order prior to, or preventing access to, the priesthood. There is now an element of freedom in exploring the diaconate as a permanent order of ministry, as in fact the post-Vatican II Roman Catholic Church has done.

Reform of the diaconate

Two possible ways ahead ought to be considered, as alternatives to the present system.

If we have regard to the role of practical assistance which the deacons gave in the early church, we should perhaps allow the office to resume that character. Let men or women be made deacons not as a stepping-stone to the priesthood, but in recognition of the charism of practical assistance evidenced in their lives. Such a ministry might be paid or voluntary. An administrative assistant, a youth worker, a hostel warden in the ministry of a large church might well be paid. A churchwarden or treasurer if made deacon might not be paid. But in either case it would be the recognition by the church's leadership of the gifts bestowed upon a person for building up the Body of Christ through practical assistance. It would not be seen as stage one in the 'ordained' ministry of the church. This would remain in the hands of the presbyters.

On the other hand, if we give more weight to the way in which the deacon was associated with the local bishop, especially in the administration of Communion, we might usefully reconstruct the diaconate in a different way. We have seen that the leadership of the local church was always plural in the early days, and that this is a healthy thing for any church. A group of experienced, reliable, local leaders in a congregation could be made deacons by the bishop, and, at his discretion and depending on need, be given licence to celebrate the Communion. This would provide a shared leadership team. It would give proper recognition to local church leaders who, unlike the vicar, will be living most of their lives in the area. It would enable a regular sacramental ministry to continue when the college-trained presbyter is likely to become increasingly rare in these days of financial stringency. These deacons would have no prerequisite or automatic intention of becoming full-time stipendiary clergy. They would remain local, theologically untrained assistants, but they could be of untold benefit in any congregation and could prevent many churches from closing or from being denied the sacraments. I foresee the day, not far away, when the college-trained leader will be the co-ordinating factor between several such groups of experienced Christians who would undertake much of the leadership of the local churches.

If it be deemed too radical and too great a break with tradition to allow deacons to celebrate, even under the bishop's licence, then let such leaders be ordained 'priests', but remain in secular employment. The Church has of course made substantial steps in this direction by allowing several ordination courses to take place locally with only the minimum of residential training, and by ordaining candidates to the Auxiliary Pastoral Ministry. They remain in their normal paid jobs, and offer ordained ministry in their spare time and of course on Sundays. This is an encouraging development, but it is not problem free. For one thing the wrong people are not infrequently chosen: they do not always come from the proven leadership of the local church but sometimes seem to be those who have an interest in church work and the time to pursue it. But there is another serious problem, that of training. Training for the Auxiliary Pastoral Ministry leaves a lot to be desired. It represents considerable extra pressure on men or women who have busy professional lives, family responsibilities, and whose ongoing responsibilities in the local church do not generally diminish. Some candidates in this training course almost become strangers to their families. Part of the trouble is that an attempt is made not to see what they really need for the ministry, but to implant in them a potted version of what a young ordinand learns in three years at theological college. Moreover, predominantly intellectual, rather than pastoral, criteria still prevail in the minds of the selectors: how many of the apostles would have been recommended for training? And often when they are ordained such people are not properly used. There is frequently no sense of shared ministry with the vicar. There is often no consultation: they are merely asked to take services from time to time at the vicar's discretion. That is not a New Testament perspective of ministry.

Whichever expedient be adopted, there is a crying need for the diaconate to be rescued from oblivion and misuse. The church cannot afford to despise such concrete embodiment of the Servant ministry.

6

APOSTOLIC SUCCESSION?

The Ecumenical Movement is one of the most re-markable developments in the church of the twentieth century. Everywhere churches are looking towards reunion, though often taking several brisk paces backwards when it seems a possibility! There are, however, three elements in the doctrine of the ministry which are proving serious barriers to reunion. Two are apostolic succession and sacrificial priesthood, and these two notions lie like submerged icebergs beneath the surface of all church unity discussions even if they are not manifestly brought into the open. The third is the matter of women priests. We shall examine these contentious issues in the next three chapters.

The place of apostles in the church

Before the resurrection

The word 'apostle' is so loosely used in current talk about 'apostolic orders', the 'apostolate of the laity' and so forth, that we need to glance at the place occupied by the apostles in the early church. That is not easy. We do not know how many there were; we know little of what they did after the early chapters of Acts; we do not know that the apostles had much to do with the administration of sacraments. They certainly baptised the first believers (Acts 2:41) but we know Paul was not in the habit of baptising (1 Cor. 1:14) and there is no evidence that they normally presided at the Eucharist, still less that a 'valid' Communion was impossible without the imposition of their hands upon the celebrant. Even the evidence that they made a habit of ordaining is less conclusive than we would like. Thus Telfer[1] finds in the New Testament 'no evidence that the presbyter-bishops could only become such by apostolic appointment, or that, when appointed, they received a laying on of apostolic hands,' and A.T. Hanson[2], in commenting on steps the apostles are supposed to have taken for preserving the ministry, asks: 'What steps did they take? Except for Paul, the only possible way in which the ministry could have been described as being perpetuated was in the presbyters of the Jerusalem church in Acts. But to describe these presbyters as successors of the apostles is absolutely fatal to the "Catholic" theory of the ministry. That is why everyone who tries to find evidence for the "Catholic" theory has to invent or discover a set of bishops (who were also called presbyters) to carry on the essential succession from the apostles to the bishops of the second century.'

One final problem is that the word 'apostle' seems to have been used for two different categories of people in New Testament days. The word means 'sent' and was conferred on special delegates sent out from a church (2 Cor. 8:23, Phil. 2.25, Acts 14:4,14, and often in the *Didache*). But it was of course used par excellence of the 'apostles of Jesus Christ', and it is with them that we are concerned.

The title is only very sparingly conferred on the twelve during the ministry of Jesus. They were primarily called that they might be with him, and only secondarily and subsequently sent forth by him to teach, heal and exorcise (Mark 3:14,15). They are represented throughout the ministry of Jesus as 'disciples', learners; they will be 'apostles' later, when their master is no longer with them. This happens in the Book of Acts when the title 'disciples' declines and that of 'apostles' becomes normal. The only exception to this reserve on the part of the Synoptists in calling the disciples 'apostles' during the ministry (John does not use the word at all) is the mission of the twelve, which is, so to speak, a dummy run for their apostolic ministry later on. They go forth clothed with Jesus's authority to do his work. Their message is his message, to proclaim the advent of the kingdom. Their role is his role, to be the Servant of the Lord and heal the sick, raise the dead, cleanse the lepers and cast out devils (Matt. 10:7,8, cf. 11:5 where Jesus's own role is precisely the same). During that mission of the twelve they are his representatives, clothed with his authority: 'he who receives you receives me' (Matt. 10:40). It is the shadow of things to come. But after that mission they become 'disciples' again, except that Luke solemnly points them out as apostles at the Last Supper when the new covenant is being inaugurated (Luke 22:14).

After the resurrection

After the resurrection the apostolic band take the place of Jesus (Matt. 28:18–20; Acts 1:8). They become witnesses to him just as he had been to the Father, and the Spirit bears witness along with them (John 15:26,27). They are led by that same Spirit into an understanding of the truth about Jesus, and so they become for the early church the authoritative interpreters of the person and work of Jesus (John 14:26; 16:13–15). Thus the apostles become the norm of doctrine in the church. 'That is why,' writes Cullmann[3], 'the New Testament attributes the same images to Jesus as to the apostles: *rocks* and the corresponding images of *foundations, pillars*. Never are these images used to designate the bishop.' So closely are they integrated with the person of their master that Cullmann can say 'the apostolate does not belong to the period of the church, but to that of the incarnation of Christ.' Indeed, so close is the identity between the Sender and the sent, that the New Testament can speak of the apostolic tradition as coming from the Lord himself. The exalted Lord proclaims through his apostles his own teaching and the extension of what he has said while on earth.[4]

In short, the apostles are historically unique and doctrinally normative for the church. Historically unique, because you cannot have more than one ground storey to a building. You cannot have more than one eyewitness generation. They afford the continuity between Christ and the church to balance the discontinuity of the ascension. Their place is unrepeatable. That is why they did not appoint other apostles in their place. It could not be done.

Not only historically unique: the apostles are doctrinally decisive for the church. The teaching of the church is the apostles' teaching, the fellowship of the church is the apostles' fellowship (Acts 2:42). They are the Lord's executors, his special delegates. They claimed this special position (see Gal. 1:6–12; 1 Thess. 2:13; 2 John 10; 1 Peter 1:11,12; Rev. 22:18ff), and this is what the subsequent church acknowledged when it canonised their writings. What is more, the subapostolic writers recognised this unique position which the apostles had. Clement of Rome says 'Christ is from God and the apostles from Christ' (1 *Clement* 42). Ignatius, his contemporary, writes 'I do not command you like Peter and Paul. They were apostles' (*Romans* 4). Bishop Serapion of Antioch wrote about

A.D. 180, 'We accept the apostle as the Lord himself.'
That attitude was typical of the early church. The
apostles were decisive for the foundation and the
beliefs of the church. What could not be shown to
derive from apostolic circles was not to be imposed
on any Christian as a necessary article of faith. We are
bound to the apostles and their picture of Jesus. We
cannot get behind it, even if we would. We believe because of their word (John 17:20). That is the historical
succession to the apostles which Jesus envisaged. But
in what other ways have the apostles successors?

Apostolic succession in the church

Four aspects of apostolic succession

There are several ways in which the question of succession to the apostles can be viewed. Looked at
from one point of view, there are and can be no
successors to the apostles. No other group of men
shared the particularity of being with the historical
Jesus on the one hand and witnesses to his resurrection
on the other. Theirs was an unrepeatable 'bridge'
function, and by definition it is unique. Moreover,
the best understanding of the apostle against his background is that of the Jewish *shaliach*, the representative
who comes with all the powers of his principal but
who, when his commission is over, cannot further
delegate but returns it to the sender. Accordingly
there was no attempt made by the apostles to appoint
other apostles in their stead.

Looked at from another point of view the apostles
have a succession – in their doctrine. Their teaching was, as we have seen, decisive for the church.
They were the privileged and inspired interpreters of
Jesus, and we cannot pierce through to him except by
means of their testimony. If we want to know what

Christianity is and teaches, to the apostles we must go. The canon of the apostolic writings is the measuring rod of Christian truth. The apostles continue to rule the church through their writings. People continue to believe because of their word (John 17:20).

Looked at from a third perspective there has been since the apostolic age a succession in the church of people who have been guardians of the apostolic deposit. Paul in the Pastoral Epistles was very anxious to see that Timothy conserved the apostolic teaching, and this was the earliest way in which a succession of bishops was justified. When Irenaeus began to value it at the end of the second century, it was not succession of hands imposed on the bishop which was at issue. It was the succession in office of bishops who safeguarded the teaching of the apostles against distortion and heresy from within the church and without. Bishops had, and continue to have, a primary task of defending the catholic faith of the apostolic church.

Looked at from a fourth perspective, there is a succession to the apostles in their supervisory role. The early church possessed, as we have seen, a settled local ministry of presbyters; it also possessed an itinerant ministry of oversight exercised primarily by the apostles themselves. We have also seen that at the end of the apostolic age, St. John is reported to have gone round Asia Minor setting up bishops to carry on this circulating, supervisory role of the churches. And very important it is. The value of a 'pastor for the pastors' is too obvious to stress, and the majority of the world-wide church has made good use of it from that day to this. Bishops are to be valued as symbols of continuity down the ages, and the focus of unity across the world church, of which they are supervisory ministers like the apostles. This aspect of the apostolic work is clearly capable of transmission: it has nothing unique and once-for-all about it.

A fifth, and controversial view

If in all these four cases there is succession from the apostles, why does the subject become so contentious in ecclesiastical discussion? Simply because there is yet another sense in which the phrase can be construed. This view claims that the apostles ordained bishops to succeed them, and that the historic episcopate, stretching back in unbroken succession to the apostles, is nothing short of essential to the church. Without such ordination it is impossible to exercise a 'valid' ministry or celebrate a 'valid' sacrament.

This view first came to the fore in Anglican circles with Newman's first *Tract for the Times* at the beginning of the Oxford Movement. The traditional exposition of the doctrine from then on has been that the threefold ministry is a divine institution stemming from the apostles and secured by an unbroken line of ordinations. The publication of *The Apostolic Ministry* in 1946, however, gave a new twist to the argument. It divided ministries into *essential* (i.e. those possessing unbroken links with the apostles) and all other ministries which were seen as *dependent*. Such a view was flattering to bishops, but damaging to the old 'Catholic' dogma of the threefold ministry.

Dix, the leading contributor to this important book, goes so far as to say that all the talk about the historic episcopate is beside the point. He recognises that Non-Conformist Churches should not be offered *episkopē*, for they have it already. He is not interested in the pros and cons of concentrating *episkopē* in the hands of a single individual; this he recognises to be unimportant, and potentially disastrous. 'What is really in question in our present discussions about episcopacy is not the episcopate at all. It is the apostolate,' he urges (p.295). For Dix, together with Kirk in the introductory essay, argued that the essence of apostolic authority is its derivation from the Lord. The principle is plain; 'as the Father has sent me, so I send you.' The commission from Jesus was passed on by the apostles to the bishops, who are the custodians of it today.

Such, in essence, was the theory: it has been immensely influential. Dix unwisely bolstered it with the doctrine of the Jewish *shaliach*. He saw the apostle, rightly, against the background of this rabbinic official who came with plenipotentiary powers from his principal: thus 'he that is sent is as he who sent him.' Disastrous to Dix's position, however, was the fact that the *shaliach* could not transmit his authority. 'We are therefore forced to conclude,' writes Dr. Ehrhardt,[5] himself very sympathetic to Kirk's position, 'that unless Dr. Kirk abandons Rengstorf's[6] theory that the apostle was the *shaliach* of Christ, he cannot very well maintain the doctrine of apostolic succession.'

There is therefore some disarray in the internal arguments by which this exclusive claim for apostolic succession through the historic episcopate has been supported by Anglo-Catholics in recent years. It is probably true that only a small minority within Anglicanism understand, believe or care about the point. But the theory is constantly adduced by a very influential and vociferous minority, so it may be as well to ask it four questions. Is it biblical teaching? Is it sound theology? Is it historically demonstrable? Is it Anglican teaching?

1. *Is it biblical teaching*? Nobody has succeeded in demonstrating that apostolic succession in this exclusive sense is taught in the New Testament; and the Church of England, for one, does not require

anyone to believe as an article of faith what may not be shown from scripture (Article 6). It is true that Barnabas and Paul are once said to have appointed presbyters in every city they had evangelised on their first missionary journey. Very likely it was their regular practice, doubtless with the laying on of hands and prayer. But we are never told the apostles had hands laid on them by Christ. We are never told that the ministry in all Christian communities had to wait for an apostle to come and authorise it. The New Testament indications, quite as much as the probabilities of the case, suggest that the first ministers in any congregation were appointed by the missionaries (often unknown folk, see Acts 8:1–4, 11:19–26) and then became self-recruiting. There was certainly a ministry at Rome and Antioch before these cities were visited by an apostle, and it is interesting to notice that when Paul left Philippi after his first visit, there was only a tiny group of new believers with no hint of any regular leaders (Acts 16); but when he came to write to the Philippians a few years later (without having visited them in between) there was a flourishing church complete with bishops and deacons. There is in the New Testament little ground for the view that apostolic authorisation was indispensable for ministry. To think in these terms is an anachronism. Not until the early third century did the doctrine of the manual transmission of the grace of orders begin to arise.[7]

Furthermore the holders of this view of apostolic succession consistently fail to recognise the diversity of practice in New Testament times. 'Primitive catholic uniformity' is nothing but a romantic myth. In point of fact, the prototype of 'catholic order' is represented by James and the Jewish church: the second-century episcopal lists mostly claim to go back to him. Paul, on the other hand, is interested in order but not in succession: he himself was in no succession. And a third discernible attitude to church order can be seen in the Johannine writings, where there are no special offices as such, and even the word 'apostle' has disappeared. The gift of the Spirit and the believers' love for the brethren replace them. There is no hint of succession in office as an indispensable element in Christian ministry.

Even if there were not this variety in the church order of the New Testament itself, the silence of scripture would be significant. If episcopacy were essential to the church, God would have made it clear to us.

2. *Is it sound theology*? The strength of this view of apostolic succession is that it takes the visible church of God, warts and all, with great seriousness. It is the society which Jesus left to carry out his work on earth. Nevertheless there are serious theological objections to the theory.

In the first place, it tends to limit the grace of God to episcopal communions, and is blind to the fact that God works just as significantly in non-episcopal churches. It simply will not do to dismiss this with talk of 'uncovenanted mercies' and the like.

Second, such a view is in grave danger of depersonalising the grace of God, and turning it into a substance which is transmitted through the correct pipeline. This is a serious declension from the New Testament concept of grace an God's personal and costly self-commitment to the undeserving.

Third, such a view leads to the conclusion that you can control the grace of God. You can organise it, domesticate it. If you think like this you run a serious risk of identifying external form with inner reality. Catholicism runs the same danger as Judaism, of supposing that the church stands by form and succession, not by inner reality and response to grace. Church authorities are always in danger of subordinating the spiritual and eschatological to the historical.

Fourth, the doctrine of apostolic succession reverses the New Testament picture of a ministry dependent upon the church. Instead we are presented with a church so dependent upon the ministry that if, in a period of massive opposition such as the Diocletian persecution, all Christian ministers had been rounded up and killed, that would have been the end of the church. Such a view borders on the ludicrous, but what else can Bishop Kirk mean when he writes 'should such a ministry fail, the apostolic church, which is the body of Christ in space and time, would disappear with it' (for the two are inextricably bound together)? [8] No, it is not merely the ordained ministry but the whole church which is heir to the command 'Go and make disciples of all nations.'

3. *Is it historically demonstrable?* Once again the answer must be 'No'. Ignatius has a very high doctrine of episcopacy but there is not a hint of apostolic succession in his writings. The *Didache* (15.1) enjoins on congregations the need to appoint *their own* bishops and deacons. Clement of Rome knows that, at Corinth, the apostles appointed a plurality of bishops or presbyters 'with a further enactment that if they should fall asleep other approved men should succeed to their ministry' (1 *Clement* 44.1,5). Irenaeus was consecrated not by another bishop but by the council of presbyters in Lugdunum,[9] and this practice of presbyteral consecration continued in Alexandria as late as the fourth century.[10] The whole idea of manual transmission of grace for orders is first found among Latin Christian lawyers of the third century, men like Cyprian, Tertullian, and later Augustine. Apostolic

succession was a legal fiction required by these legal minds to connect the growing conceptions of the authority of the clergy with the earlier days of Christianity. 'It served the Christian lawyer in much the same way that another curious legal fiction assisted the pagan civilian. The latter insisted that the government of the Emperors from Augustus to Diocletian was the prolongation of the old Republican constitution; the former imagined that the rule of bishops was the prolongation through the generations of the inspired guidance of the original apostles who were planters of the church.'[11] So much for a learned Presbyterian summary of the situation: now for an Anglican, no less learned. 'These Latin churchmen created a historical myth, the unhistorical nature of which they were secure from discovering. This was to the effect that the apostles had provided for the future of the church by creating an order of monarchical bishops. The first of these they ordained, according to this myth, with their own hands, and set them to govern the several churches with which they were concerned.'[12]

4. *Is it Anglican doctrine*? In the first place it is important to recall that the Church of England commits itself to scripture as the source for necessary doctrine (Article 6). This doctrine of apostolic succession cannot be derived from scripture, so you would expect to find nothing in the formularies of the Church of England to require its acceptance. That is precisely what you do find.

Succession is not included in the marks of the Church (Article 19). It is not mentioned in Article 23 which speaks of ministering in the congregation. The Preface to the Ordinal carefully refrains from unchurching non-episcopal bodies, while giving good reasons for the retention of a threefold ministry in our own church. 'In these our doings', says the Preface to the Prayer Book, 'we condemn no other nations, nor prescribe anything but to our own people only.'

The Reformers themselves freely intercommunicated with their brethren in the Reformed and Lutheran Churches on the continent. This practice continued for more than 200 years. Bishop Joseph Hall, who in 1618 attended the Synod of Dort to represent the Church of England, wrote in his book *Peacemaker*, 'There is no difference in any essential matter between the Church of England and her sisters of the Reformation. We accord in every point of Christian doctrine, without the least variation.' Richard Hooker, that most representative of Anglican divines, prized episcopacy highly, yet refused to conclude that it is absolutely necessary. 'The church hath power by universal consent to take it (i.e. episcopacy) away, if thereunto she be constrained through the proud, tyrannical and unreformable dealings of her bishops', and he is ready to recognise a ministry 'when God himself doth raise up any, whose labour he useth without requiring that men should authorise them.'[13]

This remained characteristic Anglican teaching, including most of the high church Caroline divines, until the Oxford Movement.[14] In the first of his celebrated *Tracts for the Times* Newman wrote of the bishop in ordination: 'he but *transmits*; and thus the Christian ministry is a *succession*. And if we trace back the power of ordination from hand to hand, of course we shall come to the Apostles at last. We know we do, as a plain historical fact . . . We must necessarily consider none to be *really* ordained unless they have been *thus* ordained.'

The Anglo-Catholic doctrine of the exclusive validity of those orders which come from the apostolic succession was something quite novel within the

Church of England. It is not doctrinally sound, scripturally based, historically reputable or part of the teaching of our Church. Indeed, the Anglo-Catholic historian Darwell Stone admits that it is impossible to argue 'that the present formularies and the post-Reformation English divines are committed to the necessity of episcopal ordination as distinct from the practical requirement in the Church of England.'[15]

The importance of the issue

It is important that these matters should be widely known in inter-church discussions. I have been engaged in many of these, and have been amazed by the way in which the Anglo-Catholic novelty of apostolic succession has been assumed by Non-Conformist Churches to be the teaching of the Church of England. It is no part of her teaching, and cannot be held to represent more than a minority view among some Anglicans. All Anglicans are committed to the value of episcopacy as a practical requirement in our Church. We are not committed to any theory about it, least of all to the view that it represents the continuation in our day of the authority of the apostles. For decades the Church of South India, though fully episcopal, was not granted intercommunion by the Church of England upon the insistence of Anglo-Catholics. It was a second-class citizen in the episcopal club because some of its clergy had not been episcopally ordained. The future in reunion lies not with imparting episcopal ordination, reordination or conditional reordination to non-episcopal ministries, but the coming together, perhaps by solemn covenanting, of churches whose members and ministers accept one another as Christ has accepted them. There is little doubt that episcopacy has a great deal to offer, as a symbol of unity and catholicity on the one hand, and as a pastoral office on the other. But it will not be accepted, nor should it be, if it comes with the implied or explicit rider that no other ministries are valid in the church of God.

While it is right to respect the views of minorities as far as possible, *is* it right to allow a view which was introduced into Anglicanism with the Tractarians, a view which led many of their most consistent thinkers to join the Church of Rome, to prejudice the reunion of the Anglican Church with her sister churches of the Reformation? And if it be argued that reunion with these churches on these terms would prejudice our eventual reunion with Rome and the Eastern Orthodox Church, this is an argument that must be resisted. For one thing these churches would prefer to negotiate with a united body rather than a series of disparate denominations. For another, they do not believe that Anglican orders are valid in the first place! They do not accept that we have the precious gift which we are so anxious to pass on to others. So reunion with other Reformation churches is unlikely to alter our future relations with Rome. There is great value in a bridge, provided it reaches both sides. But there is not much value in a 'bridge-church' as the Church of England delights to be, if it fails to reach either side. And that is precisely the danger the Church of England has been running since the Tractarian Movement alienated us from the Reformed Churches without gaining for us recognition from the 'Catholic' side.

7

SACRIFICING PRIESTHOOD?

As we saw in an earlier chapter, the word 'priest' is derived both in etymology and function from the 'elder' (*presbyteros*) of the New Testament. However, the word commonly has other associations; it means one who offers sacrifice. The Greek word for this person is quite distinct, *hiereus* (Latin *sacerdos*, from which we get sacerdotalism). This is not a matter of playing with words. It is a question of the meaning of Christian ministry.

Calvin complained of the Roman bishops that 'by their ordination they create not presbyters to rule and feed the people, but priests to offer sacrifice.' Roman Catholic theologians would not dispute this. The question is, does the Church of England do this? Is it official Anglican doctrine that priests, duly ordained in the apostolic succession, have entrusted to them the authority and power to offer the sacrifice of the Eucharist? Because this conception of the priesthood in the Church of England is undoubtedly significant in any talks concerning unity with other Churches, we must examine both the testimony of the New Testament and the historic position of the Church of England on the matter.

Priesthood and sacrifice in the New Testament

The priesthood of Christ and his sacrifice

Jesus Christ sums up in himself all that was symbolised by the sacrificing priesthood of the Old Testament. He has himself so discharged the office of *hiereus* that no other priest will ever be needed. All agree on this matter nowadays, and that is solid gain. I suppose there is hardly a priest of any learning in the Anglican Communion these days who would argue the old mediaeval dogma of Catholicism that in the Eucharist the priest offers Christ for the sins of the living and the dead. It is now, thank God, universally recognised that Christ's priesthood is final and complete, and his sacrifice on the cross for man's salvation can neither be added to nor repeated. Thus A.G. Hebert, though arguing for a doctrine of eucharistic sacrifice, allows 'the sacrificial action is not any sort of reimmolation of Christ, not a sacrifice additional to his one sacrifice, but a participation of it,' and he repudiates the 'idea that in the eucharist we offer a sacrifice to propitiate God.'[1] So far so good. It is difficult to see how any other view could have gained ground in the light of the Epistle to the Hebrews, with its reiteration of the finality and sufficiency of Christ's sacrifice (Heb. 7:23–28, 9:24, 10:1–22). 'Christ thus abolishes all further human priesthood.'[2]

Indeed, Christian priests would suffer from the same three defects which Hebrews finds in Jewish priests. They would in the first place be sinners, needing forgiveness for themselves and therefore unable to procure it for others (Heb. 7:26ff). Second, they could not offer sacrifices acceptable to God, for that involves a perfect life, and there has ever only been one such (10:4–10 and 9:12, 10:12). And third, priests cannot maintain a satisfactory relation with

God for others, because they die. But Jesus can and does save those who come to God by him, because his eternal living presence guarantees their acceptance with God (Heb. 7:25). The priesthood of Jesus is thus unique, and his sacrifice unrepeatable.

The priesthood of all Christians and their sacrifice

I suppose that, given their grasp on the completeness of Christ's sacrifice and priesthood, it is not surprising to find the absence of any priestly caste within the early church. And yet, of course, it is simply amazing. These New Testament writers were steeped in the sacrificial system of the Old Testament, and yet never once do they use the word *hiereus*, sacrificing priest, for any Christian minister. The Aaronic model for Christian ministry lay obviously close to hand. But they refused to use it. Just as the calling of the Servant originally applied to all Israel, but shrank and shrank until it was embodied in Jesus alone, and thenceforward belonged distinctively to his Body, the church; so it was with the priesthood. Originally all Israel was called to be a nation of priests (Exod. 19:6) to bring the world to God in prayer, and represent God to the world through witness. But Israel did not fulfil her function; neither did the Aaronic priesthood; neither did the high priest himself. It was only Jesus who brought God to us and brought us back to God.

But now his people share his role. They cannot, to be sure, share his sin bearing that Christ fulfilled alone and once for all. But in other ways the church can share. It realises the ideal which eluded Israel, for the church is a nation of priests (Rev. 1:6; 1 Pet. 2:9; cf. Exod. 19:6). What that means is expressed in the New Testament in terms of access, mediation and offering.

All Christians now enjoy unrestricted *access* to God. In the Old Testament this had been the prerogative of the high priest, once a year; with sacrificial blood he might venture into the Holy of Holies. Now the way into that holy place has been made available to all believers, through the sacrifice of Christ (Rom. 5:2; Eph. 2:18; Heb. 4:16; 10:19; 1 Pet. 3:18). No other intermediary is needed.

All Christians also enjoy *the mediatorial role* of the Old Testament priesthood. The priest represented God to humanity and humanity to God. Very well, that role is now taken over by the church, called to go into all the world and make disciples on the one hand; and to intercede for all people on the other (Matt. 28:19; 1 Tim. 2:1). This two-way mediation of evangelism and prayer is the solemn lifelong calling of the church, which is a 'royal priesthood, a holy nation, God's own people' (1 Pet. 2:9). It is significant that these two activities are both spoken of as priestly ministries in the New Testament (Rom. 15:16; Rev. 8:3ff).

In the third place, the church, and every Christian in it, inherits *the priestly task of offering* gifts and sacrifices to God (1 Pet. 2:5). Of course, this had always been the task of the priest under the Old Covenant (Heb. 8:3). The sacrifices of the church which the New Testament mentions are praise and thanksgiving, faith, almsgiving, a godly, generous life, evangelism and supremely the sacrifice of ourselves (Heb. 13:5; Phil. 2:17; Acts 24:17; Heb. 13:16; Rom. 15:16; 12:1,2).

Two points are to be noted about this priestly work of the church. In the first place it belongs to every Christian, not to any ministerial group. Secondly, 'Our offerings are not propitiations, for nothing that we could do could have turned away God's wrath. It is solely because of what God has done that we are able to approach him and bring offerings in which he will take pleasure. It is because of Christ's one, true, effective sacrifice offered once for all, that our unworthy oblation is possible.'[3]

The priesthood of ministers and their sacrifice

Priesthood is never associated with *presbyters* in the New Testament. Christian ministers are no more and no less priests than any other members of Christ's priestly Body. The idea of a priestly ministerial caste came into Christianity from pagan sources,[4] and was furthered by sacrificial analogies from the Old Testament. It is not until Cyprian in the middle of the third century that we find the word *hiereus* being regularly used of the Christian minister.

Furthermore, the Eucharist is never in the New Testament called a sacrifice, though of course the death of Christ, which it displays, was *the* sacrifice for sins. But the Holy Communion is not seen as one of the many things we offer to God. It is primarily something he offers to us. That is why it is called a sacrament of the *gospel*. The prime movement both in the gospel and this, its sacrament, is from God to us, and not from us to God – a form of Pelagianism which has considerable currency these days. Take, for example, this irenic but still misleading statement by Dr. Hebert, quoted with approval by the Lambeth Bishops of 1958: 'The true celebrant is Christ the high priest, and the Christian people are assembled as members of his Body to present before God his sacrifice, and to be themselves offered up in sacrifice through their union with him.' The bishops go on to say, 'We are partakers of the sacrifice of Christ. Christ with us offers us in himself to God.' Let us examine such claims.

First, when it is suggested that the church offers to God Christ's unique offering, this is a concept quite alien to the New Testament, which sees Christ as the one who made that sacrifice not *with* us but *for* us

81

when he took the world's sin upon himself at Calvary and then sat down in the place of honour and victory at the Father's right hand. We must not suppose, in order to evade this point, that Christ continues to offer his sacrifice on the heavenly altar as the church offers it on the earthly altar; this view of Moberley, Hicks and Bicknell has not one whit of scriptural support. According to the imagery of Hebrews there is no altar in heaven any more than there was in the Holy of Holies (Heb. 9:24). Jesus is not constantly offering to the Father his sacrifice once made. Chrysostom rightly says, 'Do not think because you have heard Jesus is a priest, that he is always offering sacrifice. He offered sacrifice once and for all and thenceforward he sat down.'[5] But does not the New Testament say that Jesus is praying for his people? Indeed it does, in two important places, Romans 8:34 and Hebrews 7:25. But in each of them the same rare and significant word is used, *entunchanō*. It means that Christ *is around* on our behalf, not that he is asking for our acceptance as from a Father reluctant to grant it.[6] His *presence* is his plea for us. Westcott saw long ago what it did and did not mean. 'The modern conception of Christ pleading in heaven his passion, offering his blood on behalf of men, has no foundation in Hebrews. His glorified humanity is the eternal pledge of the absolute efficacy of his accomplished work. He pleads by his very presence on the Father's throne.'[7]

Our problems here are partly linguistic. Christ does not *plead* his sacrifice in the normal sense of the word because it is already accepted and attested by the resurrection. But he can properly be said to plead it if by that is meant that his presence as the Lamb once slain in the midst of the throne is the silent plea for our acceptance. He does not *present* his sacrifice, if by that is meant that he continues to offer to the Father his sacrifice on Calvary. But he may rightly be said to present it, and so may we, if that is meant to draw attention to and celebrate the sacrifice once offered.

A second ambiguous phrase is the talk of 'uniting our sufferings' or 'joining our offerings' with those of Christ. This can so easily detract from the uniqueness of Christ's work. His sufferings were atoning, ours are not. His sacrifice removed the sin of the world, ours does not. The New Testament wisely does not speak of our 'offering Christ' or 'presenting his sacrifice'. We do not, according to the New Testament, associate ourselves and our offering of fitful obedience with his perfect sinlessness which removed the world's sin. We are indeed 'partakers of Christ's sacrifice' but partakers only in the *benefits* that flow from it, not in the *making* of it. Our self-offering is not part of Christ's self-offering, but a grateful response to his prior act.

This leads us on to an important distinction which must be emphasised if we talk at all about eucharistic sacrifice. Such language comes to us from the Old Testament. The Old Testament knew two different types of sacrifice. There was the sin offering which turned aside God's wrath, and the burnt offerings and meal offerings which were a sweet-smelling savour to God. The sacrifice of Christ fulfilled both types of Old Testament offering. Viewed as a sin offering, his sacrifice was complete and unrepeatable. Viewed as a burnt offering, it was unique in its perfection, but not in its character, for it was the pattern and the ideal of our own self-offering (Eph. 5:2). In this latter sense we do share with Christ in self-oblation. It is because Christ's sacrifice was at the same time expiatory and dedicatory, whereas ours is only the latter, that confusion arises. His atoning sacrifice is the *root* of our salvation. Our responsive sacrifice of

praise, thanksgiving and surrender are the *fruit* of it.
The two must never be confused.

It is true that in the second and third centuries
Christians often spoke of the Holy Communion, as
well as prayer, evangelism and so forth, in sacrificial
terms. But they did not suggest that our sacrifice
is incorporated in Christ's. Instead they saw the
Eucharist as the fulfilment of Malachi 1:11 and the
Old Testament meal offering. It was a 'sacrifice of
thanksgiving' which the church 'offers to God for
having made the world and all that is in it for man's
sake, and also for having set us free from evil.'[8] And
the Fathers take up the image of the Old Testament
meal-offering which was given by the leper once he
was cleansed from his disease; this is the thanksgiving
sacrifice they see in the Eucharist.

In short, the Christian priesthood is, in F.D.
Maurice's distinction (taken over by J.B. Lightfoot)
'*representative* without being *vicarial*'. That is to say,
when presbyters celebrate the Communion, they are
exercising a double representative function which, as
we saw, characterises the priesthood of all believers.
They act on behalf of the Lord when proclaiming
pardon and performing the actions with which Christ
instituted the sacrament. They act on behalf of the
people when they lead the prayers and praises and
present the offerings of the congregation. They are
acting *representatively*. They do not thereby take away
the right of the people to direct access to God, nor
of assuring the penitent of God's pardon. When the
minister acts as God's mouthpiece 'he does not
interpose between God and man in such a way
that direct communication with God is superseded
on the one hand, or that his own mediation becomes
indispensable on the other.' And when the minister acts
as the mouthpiece of the congregation, as 'the delegate

of the priestly race . . . here too his function cannot be absolute and indispensable. It may be a general rule . . . that the highest acts of congregational worship shall be performed through the principal officers of the congregation. But an emergency may arise when . . . the layman will assume functions which are otherwise restricted to the ordained ministry.' Such is Bishop Lightfoot's conclusion.[9] I do not believe that any other is consonant with scripture.

Priesthood and sacrifice in Anglican teaching

Cranmer, the architect of the Prayer Book, has this to say of Christian priesthood: 'The difference between the priest and the layman in this matter is only in ministration; that the priest, as a common minister of the church, doth minister and distribute the Lord's Supper unto other, and other receive it at his hand.'[10] Logically, therefore, he used the words 'priest' and 'minister' interchangeably in the Prayer Book. This has been done in the modern services of the Alternative Service Books, current in most parts of the Anglican Communion, and the use of 'presbyter', 'celebrant' and 'president' as synonyms for 'priest' go a long way to help those coming from backgrounds which are not Anglican.

Of sacrifice Cranmer has this to say:

> One kind of sacrifice there is which is called a propitiatory or merciful sacrifice, that is to say, such a sacrifice as pacifieth God's wrath and indignation, and obtaineth mercy and forgiveness for all our sins . . . And although in the Old Testament there were certain sacrifices called by that name, yet in very deed there is but one such sacrifice whereby our sins be pardoned . . . which is the death of God's

Son, our Lord Jesus Christ; nor ever was any other sacrifice propitiatory at any time, nor never shall be. This is the honour of this our priest wherein he admitted neither partner nor successor.

Another kind of sacrifice there is, which doth not reconcile us to God, but is made of them that be reconciled by Christ . . . to show ourselves thankful to him; and therefore they be called sacrifices of laud, praise and thanksgiving. The first kind of sacrifice Christ offered to God for us; the second kind we ourselves offer to God by Christ.[11]

With that clear distinction in mind Cranmer constructed the Communion Service. No mention of the sacrifice of 'ourselves, our souls and bodies' was made until after reception of the elements which display 'his one full, perfect and sufficient sacrifice, oblation and satisfaction for the sins of the whole world.' Our sacrifice is clearly responsive, made possible by his own.

If this was the view of Cranmer, what of the judicious Hooker? 'I rather term the one sort (of clergy) *presbyters* than *priests*, because in a matter of so small moment I would not offend their ears to whom the name of priesthood is odious, though without cause.' Hooker then explains the derivation of priest from *presbyteros* but admits that it has often been associated with sacrifice. He continues:

Seeing then that sacrifice is now no part of the church ministry, how should the name of priesthood be thereunto applied? Wherefore whether we call it a priesthood, a presbytership, or a ministry, it skilleth not: although in truth the word *presbyter* doth seem more fit, and in propriety of speech more agreeable than *priest* with the drift of the whole gospel of Jesus Christ.[12]

It would be tedious to show how this view remained characteristic of the Church of England until the Oxford Movement. This has been superbly done by Professor Norman Sykes in *Old Priest and New Presbyter*. It cannot be denied that at the Reformation the notion of a sacrificing priesthood within the church was firmly repudiated. Indeed at the ordination of a priest, the mediaeval habit of presenting the man with a chalice and patten was significantly changed. From now on he was given a Bible. It is hardly surprising therefore that Anglican orders are condemned by Rome because they lack the intention to make people priests in the sacrificial sense. The old priest has become the new presbyter. That is the position of the Church of England. Whatever the views of some of her members, a Church's doctrine must be judged by her formularies. There is no doubt that the formularies of the Church of England (the Bible, the Book of Common Prayer, and the Articles of Religion), do not favour the interpretation of priesthood and sacrifice advocated by 'Catholic' Christendom. Newman began the Oxford Movement convinced that he could, by subtle casuistry, reconcile the Articles with the Council of Trent. He later realised the dishonesty of such an attempt, and left the Anglican for the Roman fold.

The Anglican Church has a wonderful and proper comprehensiveness. It is important to show that those with quite widely different viewpoints can live and work together within a single communion, thus demonstrating that Christian love and fellowship go deeper than theological differences. But those Anglicans who do not adopt Tractarian views of the ministry and sacraments have a right to ask that comparatively recent intrusions into the historic ethos of Anglicanism should not be regarded as the quasi-official view of the Church. Neither apostolic succession nor eucharistic sacrifice will stand close investigation in the light of scripture and Anglican tradition, and they ought not to be allowed to stand in the way of an unequivocal recognition of those ministries of orthodox Christian communions which do not claim to stand within the historic succession or to be offering sacrifice in their Eucharists.

The last three chapters have been directed towards issues which rise in the Anglican Church in particular. This is obviously an important matter in England, and in the world wide Anglican Communion. But in the recent past I have been living in Western Canada, and it is apparent that the Anglican Church is both small and diminishing through age and disenchantment. Other churches are in the ascendancy, churches such as the English Establishment takes very little note of: the Pentecostal Church, the Alliance, the Mennonites. All these churches are growing in a country like Canada, while all the 'main line' churches are in decline. It is a solemn reminder that one can discuss matters like sacrificing priesthood, apostolic succession and the (supposedly) threefold ministry till the cows come home, but such introversion of the church is disastrous as well as irrelevant. The churches which realise that all Christians are called to serve, and give all their members a significant part in the ministry of the church, are growing. The churches that guard 'ministry' for a priestly cadre are generally speaking in decline. Sheer empiricism teaches us that all are called to serve.

8

WOMEN IN MINISTRY

In many countries these days the question of women
in Christian ministry has become an explosive issue.
This is a reflection of the social turmoil over women's
liberation, and whereas liberal opinion in the churches
tends to follow the liberation attitudes of society in
general, conservative opinion tends to take the position
that the Bible is against women's ministry. This is a
confused and contentious area: but it will not go away.
It is important therefore to concentrate our attention
on the biblical material and see how far it affirms and
how far it confronts prevailing social attitudes.

The background

Women were not highly prized in either Hebrew or
Graeco-Roman society. In the latter, women were
under the authority of either their father or their
husband; their education was slender; they could
not testify in a court of law, they could not inherit
property. In the Hebrew world, it was not much
different. Women had no rights, no education. They
were segregated in the synagogue and could not hold
office in it. If anything their position deteriorated as
the centuries went on, and the rabbis taught that
it was better to burn the Law than to teach it
to a woman, while men thanked God daily that

they were not created a heathen, a slave, or a woman.

However, by the first century A.D., the old religion of Rome was in decay and was being replaced with a multitude of cults from the East, some of them orgiastic and most of them giving an unhealthy prominence to women. Scandals were not infrequent and Roman society looked on them with fascination but suspicion. The teaching we have in the New Testament on women in ministry (and there is not a great deal of it) was largely directed by Paul to women in Ephesus (the Pastoral Epistles) or Corinth (the Corinthian correspondence). Both places had particular and unsavoury reputations. The goddess Diana was, in Ephesus, far from the chaste huntress of Greek folklore; she was the many-breasted fertility cult figure, worshipped with sensuality in order to gain union with the life principle and ensure fertility for the crops. Corinth was a sailors' port as well as being an Oriental city and a Roman capital. It was dominated by a hill, the Acrocorinth, where Venus was worshipped as prostitute by a thousand courtesans. It is hardly surprising that against such backgrounds the New Testament writers were not enthusiastic about encouraging feminism.

The Jesus revolution

Xenophon in the *Oeconomicus* (7ff) shows us what the lot of the normal woman was like: it did not change much in the centuries that followed. Isomachus is explaining to Socrates why his bride, aged fifteen, needs instruction in running the house. 'She had spent the previous part of her life under the strictest restraint, in order that she might see as little, hear as little and ask as few questions as possible.'

The contrast with the Gospels could not be greater. Jesus revolutionised the status of women by the way he acted towards them. The portraits of Mary his mother, and Elizabeth, mother of John the Baptist, are most sensitively drawn. In St. Luke's Gospel, particularly, we are confronted by women at every turn. Anna the prophetess (Luke 2:36–8), the widow of Nain (7:11–17), the marvellous story of the woman in Simon's house who washed Jesus's feet with her tears (7:36–50), and Mary Magdalene, from whom Jesus expelled seven demons (8:2). We are introduced, albeit briefly, to society ladies from court, including Joanna and Susanna who followed Jesus around and provided for him and his followers, sometimes at least, from their substance (8:3). Jesus bothered about the woman with the issue of blood and the dying girl (8:41–48). He noticed the widow with her two mites and commended her giving above all the public benefactors of the day (21:2–4). We find him relaxing in the home of close friends, Mary, Martha and Lazarus (10:38–42) and these figure more largely in St. John's Gospel. When the 'daughters of Jerusalem' wailed at his impending execution he showed more compassion for them than for himself (23:27–31), and at his death it was the women who remained round the cross, supporting him with love while the men ran away (23:49). The women observed how his body was laid in the tomb, and went away to prepare spices to bring with them on what proved to be Easter morning (23:55).

The attitude of Jesus to women was staggering. He did not treat them like chattels, but like equals. When asked his thoughts on contemporary divorce, so totally weighted in favour of the man, he repudiated it entirely, taking his hearers back to the 'one-man one-woman for ever' concept of Genesis 2:24. The *imago dei* lay in the harmonious interrelationship of man and woman in God's creation, not in domination of one by the other.

Women were the first witnesses of the resurrection (Luke 24:1ff), and were the first to be entrusted with proclaiming it (Matt. 28:1). Jesus revealed himself first to Mary in the garden outside the tomb (John 20:1ff). We find the women next at prayer with the apostles (Acts 1:14). They were waiting for the out-pouring of God's Spirit on sons and daughters alike (2:17) and they were not disappointed, for they too received the power, the gifts and the indwelling of the Spirit on the Day of Pentecost (2:1ff). We find them owning houses which they use as Christian worship centres (12:12). We find them, along with their husbands, selling property (5:1). Paul's first convert in Europe was a distinguished businesswoman, Lydia (16:14). Priscilla, who often in the New Testament is mentioned before her husband Aquila, joined him in instructing Apollos in the faith, and their homes in Rome, Corinth and Ephesus were centres of Christian worship and teaching. We find women like Mary, Tryphaena and Tryphosa engaging in active propagation of the Christian cause, 'labouring in the Lord' (Rom. 16:6,12). We find them associating with Paul in spreading the gospel (Phil. 4:3; Acts 18:1ff), and it is hard to imagine this did not sometimes include preaching. We find them assisting in the leadership of the church by means of the two defined roles of deacon and widow (1 Tim. 5:3ff; 9–17; 3:8–13; Rom. 16:1; Pliny *Ep.* 10.96). It is clear from 1 Timothy 5:9 that the widows were to be enrolled for service as well as being supported financially. As for deacons, the word is used both of men and women in the Greek New Testament. See for example, Romans 16:1.

And Phoebe, referred to there, was clearly a woman of substance and influence, since she is called *patrona* (the senior partner in the famous patron-client relationship in Roman society). This would have involved her in a leading role in society and as deacon she also shared in the leadership of the church. 'She has been a helper of many, and myself as well' says Paul in commendation of this lady, as she goes to Rome as the representative of the Corinthian church. Clearly, it will not do to suppose women had no role in the church of the first century.

But we can go further. Women both pray in church (which they could never have been allowed to do in Judaism) and utter prophetic messages (1 Cor. 11:5). The four daughters of Philip the evangelist all had the prophetic gift, and their fame spread far and wide (Acts 21:9). To be sure, there were dangers here. The church at Thyatira was plagued by a woman with prophetic pretensions who led people astray: she was like the Old Testament Jezebel (Rev. 2:20). This sort of person was a great embarrassment to the Christian cause, which may help to explain Paul's caution about women in ministry, not least in Ephesus and Corinth. In Philippi and Rome the problems appear to have been less.

The position of women

The position of women is abundantly clear in the New Testament. They are 'joint heirs of the grace of life' (1 Pet. 3:7). The clearest manifesto of the position of women is given by that supposed misogynist, St. Paul. 'There is neither Jew nor Greek, there is neither slave nor free, there is neither male nor female; for you are all one in Christ Jesus' (Gal. 3:28). This totally upsets the Jewish assumption of male superiority, in which, by the way, Paul himself had been reared. Man and woman are completely equal before God. But he means more than this. That equality has to have practical outworking, just as it does in the other two antitheses. If all are indeed one in Christ, the agelong prejudices must be abolished. Galatians 3:28 is the fundamental presupposition against which all Paul's other teaching about women must be seen.

There are three highly paradoxical elements in Paul's teaching about women over the range of his letters. First, equality versus subordination in marriage. Second, silence in church contrasted with ministry in church. Third, some teaching role or none. Let us look at these one by one.

Subordination?

First the question of subordination. Paul has a lovely understanding of the marriage relationship as one of total complementarity: 'In the Lord, woman is not independent of man, nor man of woman; for as woman was made from man, so man is now born of woman' (1 Cor. 11:11). Both owe their existence to the other and cannot do without the other. Male and female chauvinism is excluded, so is 'unisex': complementarity and partnership are the purpose of God for the sexes. But how can that be reconciled with Paul's teaching on the woman's subordination in marriage? In 1 Corinthians 11:3 Paul speaks of three headships: the same relationship subsists between wife and husband, between humankind (or perhaps 'the husband') and Christ, between Christ and the Father. In all three there is equality of life and subordination or differentiation of function. Christ is the 'head' over humanity: the husband is 'head' over his wife. There is nothing derogatory about this. It is paralleled by the Father's 'headship' over

Jesus. In each of these three relationships we see shared life and different roles.

In Ephesians 5:21ff Paul takes it further. To our amazement he expounds the whole relationship of man and wife in terms of 'subjection'. But there is no trace of chauvinist triumphalism. *Both are to be subject to one another!* That is what verse 21 says: 'be subject to one another out of reverence for Christ.' In other words, the wife is to treat the husband as she would treat her Lord. And the husband is to treat his wife as Jesus treats his people. And then Paul begins to spell out what this mutual subjection will mean. For the wife it will involve three things. She will *defer* to her husband as she would to the Lord (Eph. 5:22,24). She will *cleave* to him as she would to the Lord (v.31). She will *respect* him as she would the Lord (v.33). But if this is to be the proper attitude in the wife, the husband must merit it, as Christ does. He too must subordinate his own desires for the sake of his wife. The form his submission takes is different but just as costly. He must *protect* his wife, as Christ protects or 'saves' his spouse the church (v.23). He must *sacrifice* himself for her, as Christ did for us (v.25). And he must *cherish* her as his own body: that is what Christ does for his Body and bride the church (v.29). It is only to such loving self-sacrifice that the wife is told to submit. It is only self-giving love which deserves anything of the sort.

It should be clear that Paul has the highest view of marriage and the deepest respect for women. The wife is to the husband what the church is to Christ. It is impossible to go higher than that. Equally he is clear that in the family (and he is not talking about men and women as such but about husband and wife within the marriage bond) it was the task of the man, not the woman, to lead (1 Cor. 11:3; Eph. 5.22). Try it the other way round and ask yourself if he was wrong!

Silence?

Second, what about the contradictory instructions to women in church? On the one hand he allows women to pray and prophesy in church (1 Cor. 11:5). On the other he tells them to keep silent in church (1 Cor. 14:34). Or does he? Notice that in 14:34 he is speaking to wives, not women in general; the context makes this perfectly plain ('let them ask their husbands at home') although the same Greek word does duty for 'woman' and 'wife'. Is he contradicting himself flatly within three chapters? I think not.

Consider the background. Christian families from a Jewish background and proselytes too (the richest field for evangelism in the first century) would always have been separated in synagogue: the women would have been restricted to the gallery. Remember, too, that the woman had no education to speak of. All this gradually changes as the Christian movement begins to find itself. Men and women mix in the assembly for worship. And the women, who had been kept down for so long, now begin to assert themselves, particularly in asking questions. This brings disorder and delay in the worship. So Paul bids them keep silent with their chatter in church and ask their husbands at home. This is perfectly compatible with allowing and encouraging female participation in and even leading of the worship.

Teaching?

Third, how about the apparent ban on women teaching in mixed audiences, according to 1 Tim. 2:12? 'I permit no woman to teach or to have authority over men; she is to keep silent.' How can that be reconciled with what was happening in Paul's own assemblies and with Paul's own approval? The answer lies, I think, in the meaning of the word *authentein*, normally translated 'have authority over'. It is clearly a key word in this passage, and the passage is crucial to the supposedly scriptural argument that a woman must not by teaching 'exercise authority' over men. The word occurs only here in the New Testament. What does it mean?

The background of the word is one of sex and murder, not authority at all! In Greek writers like Euripides, Philodemus and Phrynicus the word is frankly erotic; the same is true of Wisdom 12.6. John Chrysostom in his commentary on the passage in 1 Timothy 2 understood it in these terms. If Paul is not allowing women in orgiastic Ephesus to slaughter men by leading them into cultic fornication through their teachings, that is a very different matter from a blanket teaching prohibition. And that seems to be the case. The Thyatiran 'Jezebel' taught people to fornicate and led them into spiritual slaughter (Rev. 2:20ff). The Book of Proverbs had been very clear that the prostitute's house was the highroad to slaughter (Prov. 2:18, 5:5, 7:27), and murder is one of the other well-attested meanings of *authentein*. In this rare word the murderous and the erotic combine. This interpretation makes sense of the whole context in 1 Timothy 2. Women are told to dress modestly in a city where there were many courtesans (vv.9,10). They must learn to live in a Christian way in subjection to the gospel ('silence'). They must realise that there is only one way to have union with God, through Jesus Christ (v.6) not through the cult prostitution they had once practised. (Incidentally, the Fathers used this rare word *authentein* to describe such cult prostitution[1].)

They must practise their faith in quiet decorum, not with the orgies demanded by Ephesian religion. The devil had 'seduced' Eve (the verb used in v.13,14 very frequently has sexual overtones): let them take care. Verse 15 might refer to the social and economic rescue or 'salvation' of these women through marriage and the family, or perhaps to concern for the illegitimate children brought into the world through their liaisons. In the Book of Wisdom reference *authentein* refers to 'parents engendering helpless souls'. Maybe Paul knew and caught the allusions of that Wisdom passage; maybe he was moved to reflect that the gospel of the Saviour could rescue not only the mother from the grip of immorality but the child from the stigma of illegitimacy. Both personalities could be healed by the gospel; and faith, love, holiness and self-control would grow in those who once were women of the streets.

It is not possible to demonstrate that this is the correct interpretation of this difficult passage. But it makes sense. It does justice to the Greek, to the thought of Paul, to the power of the gospel, and to the meretricious background of places like Corinth and Ephesus. Moreover it removes a glaring inconsistency from an apostle who clearly shared with women in ministry, and yet in this passage appears to deny them any part in it. If it is even a serious possibility, it should loosen up a great many restrictive attitudes among Christians who genuinely want to be guided by scripture in this matter. At least it will make us think again, and perhaps ensure that Christianity which was in the van of women's liberation in the first century does not remain one of the last bodies in the world of the twentieth century to allow women a significant place in leadership.

Women in ministry

Women's ministry in the New Testament

We have seen that the gospel of Jesus revolutionised the place of women. Naturally something like that would take some time to work through, particularly against backgrounds of deep prejudice. But even so, it is remarkable to see how far and how fast the early Christians moved.

Women engaged in the ministry of prayer, not only privately but publicly in the congregation (1 Cor. 11:5). That was a remarkable departure from precedent.

Women engaged in the ministry of prophecy. This had been dead for centuries, but revived at the birth of Jesus, and the New Testament is full of this direct communication by God with his people through the words of one member. Women as well as men took part in this and thus were honoured, in the prophetic role, as second only to apostles (1 Cor. 11:5; 12:28; Acts 21:9).

Women engaged in the ministry of teaching. Sometimes men have argued that women are constitutionally unable to teach Christian doctrine with balance and insight: they conclude that this accounts for Paul's prohibition in 1 Timothy. Nothing could be further from the truth. The Pastoral Epistles themselves show widows 'teaching what is good' (to whom is not specified) as well as 'training younger women' (Titus 2:3–5). Their role in teaching within the family is shown by 2 Timothy 1:5; 3:14.

Women engaged in the ministry of personal counselling. Priscilla and Aquila used their home to help Apollos to Christian maturity (Acts 18:26).

Women engaged in the ministry of hospitality. A good example of this is John Mark's mother and the way in which her home became a centre for Christian work in Jerusalem (Acts 12:12).

99

Women engaged in acts of charity: a lady like Dorcas gained a tremendous reputation for this. She seems to have made clothes to give away, in addition to other good works (Acts 9:36–41). A number of women are mentioned in Romans 16 as having laboured much in the Lord: this social involvement may have been one of the ways in which they exercised their ministry.

But they were also effective in evangelism. This is noticeable in northern Greece where women had more freedom in any case. Lydia, Euodia and Syntyche were three remarkable women in the Philippian church, and the latter two, Paul says, 'wrestled with him in the gospel' (Phil. 4:3) which must mean strenuous evangelistic endeavour.

On top of all this women could be deacons, as we have seen. Phoebe held this office in the church at Cenchreae (adjoining Corinth), and appears to have been Paul's delegate in taking the Letter to the Romans to the church in the capital. The context of 1 Timothy 3:11 and the way it is phrased makes it likely that Paul is speaking not of the wives of deacons (to whom he alludes in v.12) but to women deacons. Certainly this is how the Greek Fathers understood the verse, and we know from Pliny's letter (*Ep.* 10.96) that there was such an order in the church. Their value was immense especially in an oriental culture which required a high degree of segregation between men and women. In later times they visited, instructed and assisted at the baptism of women candidates. No doubt their role in the early days was not dissimilar.

Women's ministry now

Women could lead the prayers, evangelise, prophesy, engage in social relief, teach and hold the office of deacon in the early church, yet there remain strong objections within the Church of England to their exercising the ministry of presbyter. Several people in the public eye have left the Anglican communion as a protest against the ordination of women, and some male priests have found that they cannot in conscience serve within a church which ordains women. But without belittling conscience, is there any substantial reason why women should not be ordained to the presbyterate?

There is one obvious preliminary point to make. That is, for all their full involvement in the ministry of the early church, and for all their manifest equality with men in Christ, women do not usually occupy the front line in leadership. There were no women in the original apostolic band, and no women are mentioned as presbyters: there are women in support ministries, deacons and helpers of various sorts.

However, granted that in those days it would have been going too far too fast, and flying too much in face of social and cultural patterns to ordain women, what bearing does that have on the present situation? Should the fact that women were not presbyters weigh more with us than the fact that their position was clearly revolutionised by the gospel?

A new look at ordination

I believe that some still have objections to the ordination of women not just because of the ambiguous biblical material and confusions about the nature of Christian priesthood, both of which we have already looked at; nor just because of the clearly defined opposition of Rome and Orthodoxy. We find problems because we have got ordination wrong. Some years ago, Alan Richardson rather bleakly commented, 'to admit women to the priesthood would leave the present unsatisfactory situation exactly where it is, and would do nothing to promote the development of a wide variety of ministries which is the church's most immediate need.'[2]

However, the whole issue becomes rather more luminous if we see ordination not in terms of a threefold hierarchy but in the broader understanding of a shared and multiple local leadership such as prevailed in the corporate presbyterate of the early church. Once we recover that view of leadership, the issue of leadership becomes much less problematical. Women as well as men have clearly been given the charism of leadership by God. One of the most effective British Prime Ministers in recent years, to look no further, was a woman. In many denominations the divine charism of leadership in women as well as men, has (appropriately, in my judgment) been recognised by ordination. Even before the Anglican church ordained women, there was no ecclesiastical act they could not perform apart from celebrating the Holy Communion and pronouncing the Absolution and the Blessing. Churches which have ordained women have found that, once the novelty wears off, it is then seen as the most natural thing in the world that women should take their place alongside men within the shared presbyterate. Catholic objections that women *cannot* exercise the function of priests, and Protestant objections that scripture *precludes* it, are both seen to be invalid.

After all, why should a woman not celebrate the Eucharist, just as naturally as she exercises the other leadership roles with which God has endowed her? If, as deacons, women could preach and teach, evangelise, marry and baptise, why on earth should they not preside at the Lord's Table? The New Testament nowhere indicates who should exercise this presidency. It was natural for it to fall to a man in the ancient world, because of the cultural conditions. But changed cultural conditions both validate and necessitate changed practices where there is no theological or practical difficulty. To revert to Alan Richardson's view noted earlier, we can say that while in itself the ordination of women to the presbyterate does nothing to promote the development of a wide variety of ministries needed by the church, it does allow a wind of change to blow through some of the mustier corners of the church's understanding of ministry. This cracking of the moulds of tradition may well issue in a more biblical pattern of leadership, if we seize the opportunity.

To be sure, this departure from long-established tradition will heighten the fences between Anglicanism on the one hand and Roman Catholicism and Orthodoxy on the other. That may be inevitable in the short run. You do not neglect to do a thing simply because others you respect are not doing it. Someone needs to break the log-jam if any innovative course of action, seen to be right, is to take place. And this course of action does seem to be right. We have seen how women's ministry was validated by Jesus, and was a noteworthy feature of the early church. And we are at least beginning to see that the subordinationist attitude which the church, in common with the rest of society, has adopted towards women is part of our fallenness. It is significant that the 'subordination' of a woman to her husband (not, incidentally, to man in general) is one of the fruits of the Fall (Gen. 3:16). But in the beginning it was not so. God made man and woman equal. Woman was, in the timeless story of Genesis, taken from man's side, not from under his feet. And in the other account of creation, we are told that the divine image is reflected in man and woman together: 'So God created man in his own image, in the image of God he created him; male and female he created them' (Gen. 1:27). If we take seriously these hints of what the original purpose of the Creator was in the differentiation of the sexes – partnership not subordination, and if we realise that the chauvinist attitude which the church, along with others, has for centuries adopted towards women, is not supported by the ordinance of God but is in fact a fruit of the Fall, then we shall be grateful for these days of change when attitudes long frozen are beginning to thaw, and the complementarity of women in ministry world wide is beginning to be recognised. In due course the Roman Catholic Church, and doubtless the Orthodox, will come to recognise this. But it will happen sooner in Roman circles, partly as a result of the new oxygen brought into that body by Vatican II, and partly as a result of dwindling vocations to the priesthood in many Catholic countries among men. And if that is not the best reason for reform, so be it. God often has to use methods he would prefer not to adopt in order to bring light to his myopic children!

Of course this has produced tensions within the Church. It is still a painfully divisive issue, and not everyone will be reconciled to the measures quickly, but the dam has broken at the theological, pastoral and practical levels. The full ordination of women to the presbyterate in the Anglican Communion is a courageous and forward-looking step. Opposition to it, often professing to be Catholic, is in fact sectarian. It neglects the radical newness of Jesus's attitude to women. It neglects the fact that women may in any case do all but celebrate the Eucharist, bless and absolve. It neglects the general thrust of scripture, as Dr Mary Hayter has shown so clearly and irenically in her thesis and subsequent book, *A New Eve in Christ*. It is a reaction that is doomed to fail.

When the Church of England Synod declared that
no theological objection could be sustained against
the ordination of women, it prepared the church
for dramatic change to come. But it also signalled
that, in its corporate estimation, objection was more
a matter of tradition and culture than principle.
We must ask the question: could it not be the
case that the centuries of male presbyterate was
as culture-bound as many traditionalists accuse the
present groundswell for women priests of being?
With their orders of deacon and widow, with their
assertion that in Christ male and female are equal, the
early Christians were in the forefront of contemporary
thought in their day. The same can hardly be said
of traditionalists, either of Catholic or Protestant
persuasion, within the Church of England today.
The question arouses such passion for a variety
of reasons. Partly, because we harbour deep-seated
sexual prejudices. Partly because we are traditionalists
at heart. Partly because we confuse female presbyters
with priestesses. Partly because of the stridency of
some feminists, the lesbian lobby, and so forth. There
are many streams that feed into the river of reaction
on this issue. But, in God's time, this particular battle
is over.

And if we see ordination in the right way, as a group
of local presbyters working together in leadership, the
ordination of women should activate no alarm bells!
It will in fact greatly enrich the pastoral and teaching
assets of the team. When you come to think of it, it
is crazy that the ministry of the church should for so
long have excluded half the human race which God
made to be complementary.

But there is a further taxing issue which demands
to be settled. It is not the question of women's *ordination*, where the outcome is clear, however long in

some circles its implementation will be delayed; but the question of women's *headship*. It is all very well, the argument goes, to have women presbyters: they contribute invaluably to a mixed team, and are highly appropriate in a female community. But what about the headship of the team? Should that remain vested in the male or be open to the female?

A good deal of debate has recently been going on about the meaning of the word *kephale*, 'head' in the New Testament. When man is said to be 'head' of the woman are we to think of the 'source of life' (cf. Gen. 2:21f) or 'organ of sovereignty' (cf. Gen. 3:16, after the Fall)? It has been normal to take it in the latter sense, but the whole question is being enthusiastically discussed – for obvious dogmatic reasons. If, in verses such as 1 Corinthians 11:3, headship means 'source of life', then the last vestige of female subordinationism is removed. Instinctively, in a society which has for many centuries been accustomed to the role of male leadership and female dependency, a man reading a passage like 1 Corinthians 11:3 will feel that he is placed in a position of authority over his wife. Whether that is what the apostle meant is altogether more questionable, and in his most profound treatment of marriage (Eph. 5:21ff), mutual subordination, partnership, and self sacrifice in love is what he wants to see in Christian marriages. But even if we were to conclude that headship has some notion of authority in marriage (which is questionable) that would not necessarily imply that outside the marriage bond the woman could not be in overall charge. We happily accept it in the political sphere, the medical sphere, the educational sphere. Why not in the spiritual sphere?

Be that as it may. We do not yet have that length of perspective to be sure whether in the new mood of partnership for men and women in church leadership we are the dupes of contemporary 'liberationist' attitudes, or whether in fact the modern church has rediscovered a truth about partnership which has eluded many centuries of Christian people. Time will tell, as surely as it has solved the hermeneutical issue of whether or not women are bound to wear hats in church out of obedience to 1 Corinthians 11. But I do not want to end this brief discussion of a controversial topic on a controversial note. The main thing which the New Testament teaches is that God uses both men and women in his ministry. We need to do the same. And when both are working together in a team, it makes for a roundedness, a balance, and a maturity which one sex alone could not hope to embody.

For many years I have had the joy and privilege of working in such a team. First, as principal of a theological seminary with a dozen or so colleagues, male and female, sharing a corporate oversight. Women members of the team could do anything a man could do, with one exception. The one exception was of course presiding at the Communion, which, in obedience to the canons of the Church of England, was not open to them any more than it was to male unordained members of the staff team.

For a dozen years after that I had the privilege of being rector of a parish which had an equally shared ministry, comprising male and female, ordained and lay. Once again the women members of the team did everything the others did, apart from celebrating the Eucharist. It was only out of deference to the law of the Church of England that they did not do that. In all other ways they took their place as full and highly valued members of the team. Such partnership is theologically sound, and practically effective. It has a lot to offer to any local church.

9

CALLING AND TRAINING

I propose to end this book with two chapters of a more practical nature. The first arises from many years working in a theological college, where our task was to prepare men for ministry. The second arises from some years of practical ministry in a team situation at the heart of Oxford.

What should we look for in leaders?

We have already looked at the role of local leadership in general terms. Let us recapitulate, and add a little. Not all the following gifts will be found in any one member, which makes a shared ministry so important. But they are all requisite in the leadership of a local church.

1. *Leaders should be called*. In the Old Testament priesthood 'one does not take the honour upon himself, but he is called by God' (Heb. 5:4). This quality is no less essential to New Testament leadership. The candidates, those who train and examine them, and the church at large need to be sure of this first important issue: is there a genuine call? If there is, it will show itself one way or another. People will realise it. It will survive hard times, delays and disappointment.

2. *Leaders should be examples.* Paul said time and again 'I have showed you', 'I have given you an example', 'What you have learned and received and seen in me do', and the like. If the lives of ministers are not eloquent for their cause, nobody will listen to their words.

3. *Leaders should be corporate.* They must not play the one-woman- or one-man-priest. If they do, they will not only be flying in the face of the New Testament ideal of a corporate presbyterate, but will find themselves doing all sorts of things they were never intended to, and will be likely to rob others of their God-given place and function within the Body.

4. *Leaders should be enablers.* They must see their task to build up the saints for their work of service (Eph. 4:12). They must not try to do it all themselves, but endeavour to make themselves unnecessary because they delight to step into the background as others discover their gifts and begin to use them for the good of the Body.

5. *Leaders should be able to evangelise.* They may not be evangelists by gifts and inclination, but like Timothy must 'do the work of an evangelist' (2 Tim. 4:5). Christians are committed to the good-news business, and it is necessary for their leaders to be in it up to the hilt.

6. *Leaders should be able to preach.* A minister must 'herald' the gospel: that is precisely the word so often used in the New Testament. If the leader cannot preach, and is not prepared to allow others to do so, there is sure to be a drift away from the church.

7. *Leaders should be able to teach*. That is a requirement heavily stressed in the Pastoral Epistles. This again does not mean that the leaders must do it all themselves. It certainly does not mean that they must do it all by talking. But by encouraging private study, by helping group leaders to function, by holding debates, by using film, reading and study material, ministers must see that learning and growth in the understanding and practice of the faith go on in the congregation and in their own lives. That is going to require study of the scriptures and of the modern world as well (2 Tim. 2:15). It is going to necessitate doing battle for the truth and confronting error. All this will neither be easy nor popular, yet it must be done; (1 Tim. 4, 2 Tim. 3).

8. *Leaders should be able to shepherd*. They need to care for others. This may not be the particular talent of every individual leader, but they must see that it is done. They are called to be undershepherds in the flock, and they must discharge that responsibility (1 Pet. 5:1–5). Social concern, pastoral counselling, visiting, building up, helping people to discover their gifts – all this and much more is involved.

9. *Leaders should be able to lead*. They are called to 'bear rule', to 'stand out in front' (1 Thess. 5:12,13; Rom. 12:8). They must be able to initiate the action after catching the vision; to take risks, to encourage the congregation to bold, courageous, costly action. This is going to demand character, and decisiveness, and the ability to stimulate (and if necessary be restrained by) fellow leaders. It will involve 'up front' work in leadership of the services, of the committees and of the whole church. Leaders must lead. They may often do so from behind, like the officers in the Royal Artillery! But lead they must.

10. *Leaders should be tested*. These nine points stand out clearly in the New Testament as requirements in those who are going to exercise leadership. Is it any wonder that Paul adds a tenth, the insistence that a young or untried person should not be thrown into leadership too soon? Leaders must have had some experience. They must have given proof that God has indeed equipped them with ministerial gifts. 'He must not be a recent convert . . .' says the wise old apostle. 'Let them also be tested first . . .' (1 Tim. 3:6,10).

What are the tests of vocation?

The social context

Begin by glancing at the shape of the society in which the Christian is called to serve. In the world at large we can expect to see the growing impact of factors which are even now gnawing away at society: overpopulation; the social fragmentation of nationalism and tribalism; famine on an ever-increasing scale; developing tension between the 'haves' and the 'have-nots', both within countries and between them; the diminution of non-renewable natural resources; the accelerating destruction of our environment; the terrifying and escalating nuclear threat; and technology racing out of control.[1] In addition we shall see an increasing lack of purpose in many lives as unemployment grows and the silicon chip makes its revolution in industry. Unless we learn how to use leisure and how to relate to people better than we have ever done before, there is little hope for the world.

Moreover, we may expect to see a decline of organised religion, a growth in religious pluralism, an increasing suspicion of enthusiasm, and a relativistic concept of truth. Crime, corruption, and tension between sectors in society are all on the increase and are sure to grow. Human greed has not diminished. Aimlessness is prevalent. Privatisation is on the increase. Hedonism is the prevailing philosophy. Suicide and despair are round the corner. There is no rock on which to build. This is the type of society in which a great many Western Christians are called to serve.

The ecclesiastical context

And the church, what is the climate there? There will be far fewer clergy, as funds to support them crumble away in the surge of inflation. There will be an increase of self-supporting ministries which make no financial charge on congregations. The established churches will probably go broke. The Church of England will transform, or die. House fellowships may take over where empty parish churches leave off, and catholicity will be threatened. Clerical security of tenure will be a thing of the past. No longer will the clergy be able to count it their right to be paid. Lay ministry is bound to increase. Naturally, therefore, lay training will become crucial. But as yet there is no sign of much awareness in top church leadership that this is a priority. Few dioceses invest money, time and people in a programme of serious lay training.

We are living in a time of faster change than ever before. In the next quarter of a century the following developments in church life are highly probable. Some parishes will continue to exist, with their paid full-time staff as before; but they will be few. Cathedrals may be taken over by the State. A great many churches will be closed through lack of interest and financial support to keep them going. The Church of England may well be disestablished. At all events, it is coming under ever more severe financial pressure. Parish shares are spiralling higher as money from the Church Commissioners increasingly needs to be spent on other things than supporting the day-to-day ministry of the church. There may even be a complete cessation of central funding in due course, possibly even financial breakdown.

This need be no disaster. It might drive us back towards New Testament principles in a way that theological considerations have failed to do. Unless we make radical changes, we shall be faced increasingly with a circuit ministry, as one minister seeks to serve a dozen local churches. This will be combined with an almost total lack of pastoral oversight. Specialised ministerial teams will develop, especially in inner city areas. The majority of church leaders will earn their money from a secular job and will be non-stipendiary clergy. There will have to be a great flowering of lay leadership if the church is to survive. And it is not impossible even in England that an extreme nationalist or humanist takeover of power could bring the Church as an institution to a close.

Considerations for the assessors

In testing vocations for ministry in such a world, and such a church, here are some appropriate questions for the bishops' selectors and principals of theological colleges. They apply equally to men and women, but to avoid cumbersome language, I will use feminine and masculine pronouns in alternate paragraphs.

1. *Is she a woman of God?* Only a genuinely converted woman, deeply committed to Christ, with a strong devotional life, is going to survive and cut ice in an increasingly hostile and unsympathetic environment.

2. *What of his life?* Titus 1 and 1 Timothy 3 give shrewd and stringent criteria here. Questions like this arise: Is he overconfident? Is he quick tempered? Is

he a one-woman man? Is he over-keen on drink? Is he able to control himself and organise his family life? Is he unduly keen on his pay? Has he got an open home? Is he well recommended by churchmen and non-Christians alike? These questions all emerge from Titus 1:7ff. That same Epistle prompts others: Is he honest about his failures (Titus 3:3)? Is he likely to help in cases of need (Titus 3:14)? Is he prepared to engage in controversy for the faith, gently but firmly, and without personal bitterness (Titus 1:11; 3:2)? Is he discerning (Titus 3:9)? Unless a man's life passes scrutiny his ministry is bound to be ineffective.

3. *Can she work in a team?* Such teams of ministry are going to become more and more crucial. Is she basically a prima donna, seeking a stage to play on? Or will she be a team member, and be able to co-operate with other ministers, both male and female, other denominations, other theological positions?

4. *Can he communicate?* Has he learnt, in this media age, the way to communicate something of importance to those who have no idea of its importance? Can he detach himself from time-honoured language and imagery, from ecclesiastical assumptions and ways, and communicate the faith to those outside it? Can he write in an attractive way? Can he draw a crowd in the open air? Can he relate to people in a deprived or multinational area?

5. *Does she like people?* If not, she is going to be no use in the shepherd ministry. The learned recluse, the pompous parson is going to be of little value in the next twenty years. People are needed who will go out among a very needy humanity and get deeply involved.

6. *What of his intellectual capacity?* I do not look for brilliance or a good degree. I look for the ability to teach. That is the prime condition, other than a holy life, which we find in the Pastoral Epistles. A man must be *didaktikos*, apt to teach (Titus 1:9; 1 Tim. 3:2). Alas, many clergy are totally inept at teaching. They have little understanding of how people learn, and little sense of the urgency of teaching the faith. Just ask yourself how much effective training goes on in your church! If the candidate is to be apt to teach, he must also be apt to learn. He must be a thinker, and must be prepared to study. He needs to be in some measure a theological resource man.

7. *Is she flexible?* Many people are intransigent on peripheral matters, but soft at the centre. She should be the reverse. In a fast-changing social climate flexibility is essential; so is tenacious commitment to the faith. It is this skilled adaptability that is so rare and so necessary. The church at large has failed signally here. Either clergy have been avant-garde and distanced themselves from the historic faith, or else they have stuck punctiliously and unimaginatively to the way it was expressed in previous generations.

8. *Has he got vision?* Particularly, he needs a vision of the Body of Christ in a given area, with every member working properly. Has he the determination to see this vision carried through into reality? Is he likely to be sensitive to perceive new needs and new opportunities as they arise? Or is he an 'as it was in the beginning, is now, and ever shall be' man?

9. *Is she prepared to sacrifice?* She will be called to this in the area of money, time, family, ambitions and

probably persecution. If she is weak on sacrifice she is going to be weak on the servant ministry, which is the only ministry worth having in the church of the Servant.

Questions for the candidate

So much for testing vocation from the point of view of those called to train. What are the indications for the possible candidates? How can they begin to sense the call of God in this matter?

1. *She must be willing to do anything.* It must be 'Teach me thy way, O Lord,' not 'Bless my way, O Lord' (Ps. 27:11). Only when we are totally open to God's guidance can we expect to receive it.

2. He would be wise to expose himself to a variety of circumstances, so as to see and develop gifts which at present he may have no idea he has. God does use circumstances to guide us (Acts 16:9,10).

3. *She must examine the scriptures.* Not so much for proof texts, though on occasion God can and does guide by illuminating some particular verse. But the general thrust of scripture can be of enormous value in disciplining and directing her thought processes, so that she begins to have the mind of Christ and think as Christ would think about contemporary issues, including her calling.

4. *He must assess his capabilities.* Charles Spurgeon had a wise saying: 'If God calls a man to be a preacher he gives him a big chest!' In other words, where God calls he equips. If God is calling him to leadership in the church, then there will already be some indications in the way he is blessing the man's ministry at present.

116

Incipient gifts of ministry will be evident in his life.

5. *She should consult others.* Not that others are necessarily right, but if it is God's will that she should exercise ministry in the congregation it is probable that others will have noted the possibility too and will encourage her to press ahead and knock on the door to see if it opens.

6. *He should consult his own heart's longings.* God is not an ogre. He delights to 'give you the desires of your heart' (Ps. 37:4). Let him not make the mistake of supposing that if he wants to do a thing it cannot possibly be the will of God.

7. *She should expect a growing inner conviction.* If it is a real call from God it will survive the douche of cold water, the ecclesiastical delays, the problems along the way. It will welcome tests as confirmations, or the reverse, of what has seemed to be a call.

Those are some of the considerations to bear in mind when considering whether or not God is calling us to a ministry of leadership in the church. We should beware of dogmatic utterances from others; of impulse in ourselves; of supposing that in this very needy world the recognition of need necessarily constitutes the call of God. It does not. There is need everywhere. What matters is that between them the candidate, the local church and the wider leadership of the church of God come to a common mind about where and how this particular limb within the Body of Christ should find his or her main sphere of service.

How shall we train for ministry?

All Christians are called to serve their Lord, the church, each other, and society. Once this basic biblical truth begins to be believed, taught and acted upon, ecclesiastical hearts will beat less irregularly at the rise and fall of numbers offering for 'the ministry'. Leaders will emerge in each local area, and be recognised by the church through ordination. Some of these will probably be trained locally on the job. Others will continue, as at present, to have at least part of their training in a residential college. Some will derive their income from continuing in secular work. Others, particularly those with special gifts which cry out to be used more widely than in a single congregation, may well be paid as full-time workers. But the day of appealing for vocation to *the* ministry will have ended. Instead will come steady teaching in each congregation to encourage every member to seek God's call for the area of work within which to exercise most effectively and usefully the charism God has bestowed.

The variety of leadership which the New Testament leads us to envisage in a healthy church sets a high premium on training. This the Church of England has handled with such an obvious double standard that its real assumptions about ministry are painfully obvious. Despite the recent closure of some theological colleges, and lower numbers of people accepted for training, the Church still spends a vast amount of money on the equipping of relatively few ordinands. At the same time, although the amount is increasing, little is spent on lay training. Yet more and more parishes are grouped frenetically into larger and larger units, and fewer and fewer stipendiary clergy circulate in ever faster circles. It seems to me, therefore, that we are called to consider training of three types.

118

Training local presbyters

First, we must train local presbyters. These will, if we follow the New Testament, be tried people of experience. They will be men and women who have shown gifts of ministry: some administrative, some teaching, some counselling, some evangelistic. Together a group of them will be able to constitute an effective all-round corporate presbyterate. They might fittingly be ordained by the bishop once he is satisfied of their competence to lead in the local situation.

This competence is partly gained by book learning, but it is gained much more from experience. This is where the value of shared ministry shows itself. Within the corporate presbyterate there will be many skills on offer. New candidates will learn a great deal by apprenticeship to more experienced colleagues. That, after all, is how the church has trained its ministers down the years. The Timothys got trained by the Pauls, not by taking them away and putting them in colleges. There is a great value in college life, but it is not best fitted for training local leaders for the practical ministry.

The local presbyterate will naturally meet regularly: probably early in the morning, if many of them have secular jobs. This team will learn from one another and from scripture, from experience, from the occasional presence of some Christian leader from another part of the country or the world who happens to be in town.

Some at least of the training could be in co-operation with a local theological college or even a university department. I foresee a great increase of theological education by extension, which has proved so valuable in Latin America and India. This means that the college comes to the candidates, not vice versa. One or more central experts, from a college or elsewhere, come to train local leaders on the spot.

With the growing sophistication and decreasing cost of television we can look forward not only to high calibre teaching being filmed on video and played from cassettes, but to the possibility, already happening in Christian education in America, of having the teachers available for questioning by pupils on television, by means of satellite. The development of the silicon chip means that the next twenty years are likely to be even more revolutionary in the area of audio-visuals than the previous twenty years have been. Is the church at large going to wake up to the enormous possibilities of widespread Christian education which technical advances have made possible? Or will it, ostrich-like, continue to depend on the preaching and teaching gifts of the one local pastor, who may well have had little training in this vital area of Christian communication?

However, once the need for training is seen, and the facilities grasped, the local situation, weak as it currently is, could be transformed in a few years. Through reading, through courses held in the local church, city wide, and on T.V., Christians could grow in understanding. By practical involvement in local ministry, and sometimes by going out in teams to visit other churches, the budding local leadership could be 'earthed' and equipped for useful service.

Jesus trained his followers by apprenticeship. They *saw* him work, then *shared* in his work, then *did* it themselves, then *trained* others. The church greatly needs to recover this pattern of training a group of leaders in each congregation. Among other benefits, there would no longer be the hiccups and policy changes associated in many a parish with the arrival of a new vicar. Instead there would be the gradual development of a leadership team, able to offer more effective and stable all round ministry in the church; able also to survive the departure of a vicar without hiatus.

Whether or not ordination to the local presbyterate should continue to be for life would, no doubt, be hotly contested. If not, the authorisation could be for a limited and renewable period. If a lifelong concept of ordination continued, there would be need for a strict exercise of the diocesan licence to officiate. This would enable any mistakes to be rectified, and would also mean that if a presbyter from one area moved to another, leadership would not be exercised by the presbyter unless and until the call came from that particular church to join their team. Leadership would then be a right that was earned, and this could be recognised through licensing. Needless to say, this local training and equipping of new presbyters through membership of a corporate body would be infinitely cheaper than our present expensive and élitist method of training.

Lay training

Second, we must concentrate on lay training. I do not like the word, for reasons expressed above. There are not two classes within the church. All are called to serve. And that is just what these lay training courses must show. Congregations do need training to see themselves as the Body of Christ, where all are expected to contribute to the whole such gifts as God has entrusted to each. There needs to be training in the faith, training for new converts, training in marriage and parenthood, training for different areas of ministry within the church. A comprehensive scheme of Christian education needs to be undertaken regularly.

It may well be that despite the different church habits in Britain our congregation could adapt and greatly profit by the all-age Sunday School which is a feature of American Christianity. This means that a series of courses is provided, and members of the congregation go not only to worship service but to one of these courses as well. Certainly the standard of Christian education in most British congregations is deplorably low. The average Christian today probably knows less about the faith than the reasonably competent Sunday scholar half a century ago.

Naturally, the local presbyters will receive this education as well as being among the dispensers of it. This is worlds away from the current supposition that the clergy know it all (or are supposed to know it all) already. They do not. There are members of congregations who have specialist skills to teach in the local church – skills in counselling, ethics, science and religion to which most clergy are comparative strangers. These resources urgently need to be tapped.

There is need for a wide spectrum of continuous Christian education in the local church: in country areas, this could be done at deanery or market-town level and preferably interdenominationally. As members of the congregation get into these training courses, begin to relish them and learn from them, they will discover and use their gifts. The result will be a growing number within the local church of people who are using their talents for the Lord, and thus a growing cadre of potential presbyters for the future. If a massive education scheme like this is to be undertaken (and it is crucial) then dioceses will need to finance it, and themselves have the humility to learn how it can be done effectively. There will need to be new attitudes in the pew and among the clergy. But it can be done. In places it is being done. When it is done, the church comes alive.

College training

The third training area is, of course, the theological colleges. These have been pruned in recent years, and those which remain are now offering a better training than previously. All college staffs know the problems and the strains. The curriculum keeps increasing while nothing offers to drop out! The training, being residential, is inevitably more academic and less practical than would be desirable. The academic aspect therefore assumes more importance in the minds of staff and students alike because it is more readily assessable. At present it is very hard to 'fail' unsatisfactory students if they have negotiated their selection procedures and manage to pass their academic exams. Ordination is seen as the carrot to encourage the student along the road. All of these things, and many others, add to the frustrations of a theological college teacher.

But if most of the local presbyters were trained on the ground a good many of these problems would disappear. The college would continue to be of the utmost importance. It would be the place where the most rigorous examination of every side of the faith and life of the church took place. It would be the place where some of the local presbyters would undergo short or longer course training for special purposes. It would have a small number of young people taking honours and advanced degrees with a view to becoming the scholars and academic leaders of the church in the next generation. Its staff would themselves become a corporate leadership which could offer a model to others throughout the area. They would at certain periods of the year run refresher courses and at others go out to offer theological education by extension courses.

It is the colleges, rather than the universities, which

need to become the seedbed for the intellectual leadership of the church. Universities are increasingly setting up departments in the phenomenology of religion, and moving away from departments in Christian theology. That move will accelerate under the influences at work in our society, and the church must react accordingly, by placing less and less reliance on university departments for the training of church leadership, and also by encouraging the most able students to devote their skills not to writing doctorates on minutiae which are of little significance to the church, but to building up the leadership of the next generation. And what could be more worthwhile than that?

Such a use of theological college resources and personnel would enable the staff to have a much greater contact with and influence on the life of the churches at local level. It would make a far greater use of their gifts and expertise which would be made available, through extension courses, to far more people. The college would be used for short-term as well as long-term candidates, with ordination no longer being the inevitable goal. For the training would not be for the untried, but rather for the further equipping of those who have already received some training at local level, and are already displaying gifts of leadership in the local church.

These are some of the ways in which theological training in the future could better serve the corporate local leadership of the church of the Servant. The question is, will we dare to be radical enough while there is still time?

BUILDING FOR SERVICE

Scholars have often discussed why the twenty-first chapter of the Gospel of St John was added to what seems to be a completed book. After the confession of Thomas and the words of encouragement uttered by Jesus to those who have not seen and yet have believed, it is surprising that a further chapter ensues: there is almost a sense of anti-climax.

It is perfectly possible that the Gospel at first circulated without chapter twenty-one. But it was soon added, and almost certainly by the same author with the commendation and encouragement of his Christian friends ('we know that his testimony is true' John 21:24). Why was it thought necessary?

Partly, no doubt, to show Peter's triple reinstatement by Jesus after his triple denial. Partly, possibly, because it was necessary to counter rumours that the 'beloved disciple' had been told by Jesus that he would not die but survive until the parousia. But surely the main purpose of the chapter is to show the threefold task of the church that Christ left behind to carry on his work. They must catch fish (vv. 1–14) and they must feed sheep (v. 15ff). The making of disciples and the training of disciples are the two major aspects of the ministry of Christ in the world. The role of leaders is the third strand in this chapter which is inseparable from the other two: they must be both partners and enablers.

We have looked at the theory of Christian ministry a good deal in the previous chapters of this book. Now I want to recount, diffidently how my colleagues and I attempted to carry out those principles in one parish, and in many ways a very peculiar one. It was situated in Oxford. Half the congregation were undergraduates, who lived in Oxford for only half the year. We were short of families, in common with many city centre churches. We were an international area. We had very antiquated and inadequate buildings. It was by no stretch of the imagination a typical parish and the application of the principles of ministry there was inevitably very different from the way things would work out in a more 'normal' parish. Nevertheless, the principles themselves have withstood a good deal of testing down the years; evangelism, training, body life, shared leadership are four principles of leadership which can and should be applied anywhere. But I do write diffidently, because it would be very misleading to suggest that we succeeded in the ministry which God set before us in such an exciting situation. There were many encouragements. Many people were won to Christ. Many went into their careers (some of them top-ranking careers) determined to make Christ their Lord and Master. Many were ordained, and others became missionaries, both from the 'town' congregation and from among the students. There was a good deal of mutual love flowing in the home groups of the parish to which nearly everybody belonged. Teams went out from the church to minister in various other parts of the country. But all was not rosy. We had the headquarters of the police and of the civic authorities in our parish, and made precious little impact on either. We had a purpose made youth club, which in the days of the 'skinheads' in the 1960s had been crammed with young people. But despite all sorts of attempts we failed to make it an effective instrument of the gospel in the 1980s. The city centre of Oxford is also full of homeless men, many of them alcoholics and unemployable. We fed them, but we did not manage to achieve an effective work for God among them: to our shame, we often felt they were a nuisance. Nor did we succeed in making any difference to the unemployment scene in the city, hard though we racked our brains to try.

So it is emphatically not from any sense of triumphalism that I write what follows. But unless a book such as this is grounded in genuine practical experience, it is very easy to dismiss the principles as unrealistic, or at any rate incapable of application within the structures of the Anglican Church.

The making of disciples

If the church genuinely does exist for the benefit of those who are not yet its members, strenuous efforts must be made to reach them. The church at large has a bad image, and this assuredly will not be overcome if congregations continue the way they are. A definite initiative is required.

1. *First comes the ministry of prayer*. Without that, nothing happens. Unless we are praying for people to come to the Lord, praying regularly and corporately and imaginatively and in faith, we shall not see very much. Therefore a parish prayer meeting of some sort is a necessity. It may happen in silence. It may happen by prayer in groups. It may happen at a central prayer meeting. It may involve prayer

breakfasts, prayer partnerships, nights of prayer. But the ministry of prayer is clearly crucial for the growth and deepening of any church.

2. *The church must be seen to care.* So often it appears as a private hobby. Like a gardening club the church seems to be a society bent on its own preservation, but without paying much attention to others. Yet if it is to cut any ice, it must be seen to care about the quality of life in the area and the problems folk wrestle with. For instance, it may need to contend for the supply of playgroups, or fair shares for racial minorities in such employment as is available. It may start, and staff, an adoption clinic, as an alternative to the evil of abortion. Whatever the problems that affect the life of the community, the church needs to be seen to care for the good of those who are not its members: Jesus did.

Unemployment is one of the scourges of our day. The church needs to be seen to be concerned, and involved. It may launch a job creation scheme. It may run a coffee bar for disenchanted youth. It may initiate a night shelter for homeless teenagers. It may be involved in the housing of those with nowhere to go. It may bring into being a restaurant or coffee house where people can rest and eat, be surprised at the quality of food and love – and then discover it is run by the church. Care shows itself in a thousand ways. Unless it does, however, evangelism will prove fruitless.

3. *The church must be a friendly place.* The average public house is much more friendly than the average church. Church people underestimate the fear and prejudice against even entering a church building which inhibits millions in this country. Therefore friendship is the great way of breaking down barriers and demonstrating the Servant ministry. A simple

expedient like having people greet one another for a five-minute 'buzz' at the start of the service; the serving of coffee afterwards; the ready invitations for visitors to have a meal or spend a night – these things make a profound impact, the more so because, to our shame, they are generally unexpected. In the case of students, Christians at Oxford University write to every single freshman and woman before they come up to the university. They offer friendship and invite them, if they wish, to the Christian fellowship. Many new students are met by Christians as they arrive, and are helped to settle in. Several of the churches offer a free lunch to all new students at the university. In ways like this a seed is sown – if only of curiosity.

4. *Evangelistic preaching in church* is something which every church could and should do at appropriate times in the year. If there is any regular turnover in the congregation, it is a fair assumption that some at least will not have a personal Christian faith, but will be visiting the church in a spirit of enquiry or mild interest. On three or four occasions in the year we have a well-prepared, well-advertised evangelistic address which is designed unashamedly to help people to repentance and faith in Christ. The worship, the music, the employment of appropriate aids such as dance, drama, banners and testimony may be useful, and they are all subordinated to the one aim of drawing men and women to Christ. At the end of the service an opportunity is given for those who so wish to stay behind and entrust their lives to Christ. They are interviewed within the next twenty-four hours and directed into groups for new Christians.

5. *Evangelism outside church*. Evangelism need not be confined to set pieces in church. We find that

other settings are often preferable. We have engaged
in it at supper parties in people's homes: after the
meal there is an opportunity to give an arresting
talk on some aspect of the faith and take comments,
criticisms and questions from those present. This often
is very fruitful, particularly if the party has a certain homogeneity – sportsmen, for instance, or young
couples. A major enterprise, carefully planned, using
the Town Hall is another means of outreach. One
could use a musical evening with a Christian artist
who both sings and speaks about Christ; or a debate
between a well known Christian and non-Christian; or
a seasonal event such as a pre-Christmas multi-media
presentation. The value of high quality presentations
is considerable and they often have a great impact. In
the Oxford colleges it is often possible to respond to
invitations to speak in somebody's rooms or a lecture
hall; better still in the college bar, with the assistance
of some dramatic sketches and testimony from the
students in that college. A recent summer development in Oxford which proved very fruitful was an
evangelistic strawberry and Pimms' party in a college
garden, complete with music to match! There is no
end to the ways in which the gospel can be shared,
naturally and without embarrassment, if we have the
imagination and motivation to get involved.

6. *Debates have their place too.* All too often the Christian case is insulated from come-back because of the
privileged position given to the sermon. But if it *is*
the truth of God, it can withstand confrontation and
opposition. I have found that a debate with a leading
secularist on the nature of man, or with students on
free sex, or with communists on goals for society, or in
a debating society on the evidence for the resurrection
of Jesus – these things all draw a crowd, composed

largely of those who would not go to normal Christian
gatherings. Sometimes people discover Christ through
only one such presentation. More often they are set on
the trail of enquiry: reading, arguing, and thinking,
which can in due course lead them to faith.

7. *Open-air ministry* is generally thought to have
had its day, at least in fairly sophisticated locations.
This could not be further from the truth. Wesley
and Whitefield changed the face of England through
open-air preaching in the eighteenth century. We find
that the presentation of the Christian message in the
open air remains both enjoyable and effective in the
twentieth. Not, of course, if it is delivered by a mourn-
ful person at a street corner exhorting the audience
to repent and meet their God! But if a large group
gathers in a well-populated place – a high street,
a shopping precinct, a beach – and proceeds with
humour and joy to speak of Christ inductively, taking
a cue from the situation prevailing at the time, it can
cause great interest. People don't expect it. They imagine that Christians will keep to their churches. But
if we have good news, why should we stay confined
to our buildings? Jesus was an open-air preacher; why
should his followers not be?

Three factors help enormously in open-air work.
The first is dance. We use Israeli group dances in
the streets and this amazes people. 'What have these
people got to be so happy about?' is their question,
spoken or unspoken. Once that question is lodged
in their minds, the speaker's task is made so much
easier – simply to tell them what accounts for this
joy. Equally, short dramatic sketches often seem to
get through to places where the ordinary spoken word
does not reach. They are a most powerful medium,
and if some of the congregation see it as their Christian

ministry to write and rehearse such playlets, it will be of great value for the spread of the gospel. A third asset is the use of visual material. Jesus preached continually from the things all around him, and used them as vehicles to draw people to God. We can do the same, and we should. A particularly effective way to do this is by means of a sketch board. It immediately draws a crowd, and those who are really interested stay on for personal conversation.

Always the most valuable part of the open-air work is the conversations which begin round the edge of the crowd. These often ripen into something more, and lead to interest and sometimes to conversion. Even when things do not go that far, a nice taste in the mouth is left behind: people see that the church can come out from behind its fortifications, that it is not dull, but is comprehensible and happy. If that impression has been created, time has not been wasted.

8. *A period of mission*. This can take many forms. It may be a weekend of Christian apologetics and evangelistic preaching put on by some church either in its own building or on common ground. It may be a full week-long event, carefully prepared for over a period of time. We engage each September in a fortnight of mission with a church or series of churches in a town, taking a team of 80–100 with us. They do not all preach, of course: many of them are young and inexperienced Christians. But their common life, their love for Christ, their willingness to have a go, their imagination and hard work speedily endear them to the local Christians who are encouraged and stimulated. The Body is seen to be operating in every part, and in love. There are house meetings, much visiting, teaching in schools, factory visits, entry into prisons and borstals, and of course central meetings

and youth events, together with preaching and speaking at all levels in the churches on Sundays. In ways like this many people come to a living faith, and this is as much encouragement to the visitors as it is to the local Christians. The shared enterprise of mission brings fellowship and much joy.

9. *Personal evangelism*. At the other end of the spectrum from a public event like the large mission, personal evangelism is almost a hidden ministry. Here one friend takes another friend to church or a meeting – or they simply find themselves talking about the things of God. If members of the congregation have been schooled in how to lead another to faith, there will be enough basic knowledge there for the Holy Spirit to use. We certainly find that a good many people each year come to Christ through the personal conversations they have had with one or more Christian friends; this is a more effective method than preaching or big meetings, because it enables enquirers to come out with what is really bothering them and proving an obstacle to faith. In the first chapter of St John Jesus himself led a string of individuals to faith in this way, by personal and very natural conversation. It is a ministry to be coveted, and training needs to be offered within the congregation. Then there will not be undue reliance on the ministry of the 'professional'; ordinary church members will find to their great delight what a privilege it is to lead someone else to the feet of Jesus. They will then have a great zest to do it again!

The training of disciples

Believers in Christ embark on a life of obedience. Some evangelists too readily forget that Christ calls people not so much to decision as to discipleship. How is a church to conserve and build up the results of its outreach?

1. *Agnostics' Groups*. Perhaps we would do well to begin one stage further back. In St. Aldate's we found it useful to arrange small groups for people who were unsure about the Christian faith and were prepared to consider the evidence. Sometimes these Agnostics' Groups were run by one or two experienced Christians and, say, ten agnostics; sometimes on a fifty-fifty basis. Sometimes the group worked out its own agenda, sometimes it went through a book like C.S. Lewis's *Mere Christianity*, or tackled basic issues, one each week. The purpose of a group like this is to help members discover their way to Christ by removing difficulties and objections along the route. This requires understanding, patience and empathy. It is important to expose people to scripture, which has its own power, even when folk profess not to believe it. A meal and friendship are important ingredients in forming trust and promoting openness. The loan of books on different aspects of Christian faith and behaviour can help; so can the companionship of other Christians and the testimony of those who have recently been agnostics themselves.

Such groups ought to be a common feature in the churches of our land, but in my experience they are rather rare. Why so? The clergy are supposed to be trained in the content of the faith and other world views; this should be the sort of group in which they might be expected to excel. But it may be that other members of the congregation have greater gifts in this particular and exacting ministry. No matter by whom, this is something that needs to be done on a widespread scale in a post-Christian country like Britain. Non-Christians are not going to come to a church; the church must come to them. Christians must engage them in open discussion in home or pub. It is hard work, but very rewarding. I have found that a good half of those who commit themselves to this eight-week course of enquiry in an agnostics' group become Christians before the end of the course.

2. *Beginners' Groups*. From the Agnostics' Group or from personal or churchbased evangelism, the Beginners' Groups were stocked. St. Aldate's depended heavily on these for the nurture of new believers. The church had the peculiarity of being set in the midst of a continually changing open-minded group of intelligent and enquiring young people: but every church that expects to win new believers needs to work out an appropriate means for their nurture. Coming to church is not enough: it will probably be a totally strange world for them, to begin with. Attachment to a church house-group will normally not be a good idea initially either. New believers would start a long way behind the others, and be intimidated. They are full of doubts and questions, and need careful and specialised attention. A Beginners' Group consists of two or three leaders and a dozen or so new believers (or those seeking a refresher course in Christian basics). Each week they examine some important area of the faith – assurance, prayer, the church, the Holy Spirit, the Bible, the person of Jesus, and so forth. The way in which each subject is handled will depend on the group. There may be an introductory talk; there may be a guided study. There may be a supper shared, a verse of scripture memorised. There will probably be a bookstall. There will certainly be a time of sharing of joys, discoveries and problems; and there will be a time of Bible reading in a small group followed by prayer. Each person

shares what they find most helpful in the passage, and often the discussion is lively and highly relevant to life. They learn to pray, shortly and simply, at the end of each evening, though this may be a totally new experience to them. Notes are given out as they leave – and often it is midnight before they do!

They have learned so much even after one or two such evenings together. They have discovered Christian fellowship in the small group; they have found out that others have problems like themselves; they have found that the Bible speaks, and have begun to learn from it; they have gained insight into the theme of the evening; they have begun to pray in the company of others and discovered its joy and strange power for linking people in fellowship. They have discovered that by their stumbling comments they help one another; they begin to make Christian friends in the group; they start the habit of verse learning and reading Christian books; they are no longer embarrassed to talk about their own spiritual discoveries and doubts. A great deal goes on in the dynamics of these small groups. In addition, new Christians will need help with their devotional life and with the worship and the behaviour of the Christian family into which they have come, so they will need one or two individual sessions with one of the leaders. They may well need to be baptised or confirmed, in due course. A weekend away for the group at the end of the course (which might profitably last two months), is invaluable in binding folk together, and consolidating the work that has been done.

3. *Fellowship Groups.* Those graduating from Beginners' Groups are now ready for the basic cell structure that permeates the whole life of the church: they are often known as Home Groups or Fellowship Groups.

Christians need the support not only of the large or formal church body, but also of the informal small group, preferably based on geographical location. In such a group each person is loved and valued. They learn to belong, and are missed if they are not there. These groups meet weekly or fortnightly, depending on the other structures within the church. Anything more infrequent than a fortnightly meeting is too little for the group to grow together in fellowship and real openness with one another. Ideally all members of the congregation will be part of one of these groups; in practice not more than half or three-quarters of them will.

These groups become the basic pastoral units in a church. The members do indeed bear one another's burdens and so fulfil the law of Christ. Problems are shared, joys celebrated, the scriptures studied and applied, and sometimes the group has a night out for recreation, or goes to paint some particular person's room as an act of love and fellowship. The members get to know and love and depend on one another. Close friendships develop. Several groups have extra breakfast meetings for prayer and companionship. And from time to time the whole group will go away for a weekend to relax, or for service in a church or mission situation. They become, in short, 'the church in the house' in these midweek gatherings, and 'the church gathered' on Sunday.

There are, of course, other groups in a church like St. Aldate's, but they all share in this 'Fellowship Group' concept. For instance there is a banner-making group, a dance group, a youth group, a women's meeting, a drama group, a choir group: but one and all are determined not only to engage in the particular activity which draws them together, but to adopt the role of the servant to one another, and so grow in partnership, love and unity. And this is one of the most attractive features of any Christian church; when its members manifestly love each other and the Lord very much. It shows. And it draws.

4. *Training Courses.* Training takes many forms, but a programme of continuous training is essential in a church that takes its servant commission seriously. Most churches have some form of training for confirmation, the baptism of adults, and the parents of candidates for infant baptism (though, scandalously, these are still by no means universal). But there it ends. The ignorant and willing are generally recruited for Sunday School teaching, but rarely trained! Christian education in the round is scarcely attempted in the Anglican Church, and the low standard of sermons, or rather, sermonettes, is not calculated to make for much growth. We need to take great pains with the training of one another in the congregation: we must build one another up.

The way in which St. Aldate's attempted this training was somewhat as follows. From time to time we had training courses for various needs; for counselling, for marriage guidance and preparation; for mission; for leaders in youth work; for thinking in a Christian way. For the most part these courses were of short duration – up to ten weeks or so. But increasingly we discovered that a concentrated time away, be it a day, a weekend or a week was far more effective for training purposes than an extended course involving an evening a week.

Moreover, Christian students in a particular discipline, whether politics or medicine, engineering or theology, tended to get together and discuss how their faith impinged on their academic discipline. This could just as effectively be done on the shop floor by

Christian shop stewards, or by NCOs or officers in an army unit. This can be a real learning occasion, even though there is no formal teaching. It is part of training the church.

In St. Aldate's we put on, during term time, a Sunday lunch for those who liked to stay on after the morning service. Numbers were usually around 80–100. It was a marvellous opportunity to meet and greet new faces: it was a chance to quiz the preacher on the sermon, and to take steps to apply it. A gathering like this can be a real learning occasion.

5. *Training for mission* ought to be included. Each year we took around a hundred members of the congregation – in our case mainly students – away for a two-week mission in some part of the country to which we had been invited by the local churches. The host had been engaged in preparatory house groups on an inter-church basis for a whole year. Such a mission was extremely good for us. It enabled our members to share in the spreading of the gospel and to see it taking root in new lives among ordinary people. And it was good for the parishes to which we went. They got drawn together ecumenically by the venture, and they received converts after the mission was over. Naturally such a mission cried out for training before we went, and this we attempted to do by an eight-week course and a preparatory visit to the town.

As our experience grew we realised the value of a public celebration of the Christian faith, bringing together all the churches in a town, and having a major focal point each night, along with street parties, open-air dance and drama, school visits and so forth. This enabled a lot of teaching and mutual building up to take place; many barriers were broken down and inhibitions laid to rest. There was generally some evangelistic by-product as well.

A venture like this imparted something of the flavour of Christ to a whole town. While the 1981 Toxteth riots were going on in Liverpool, not far away, in Shipley, churches of all denominations joined with us in celebrating the faith for a week with large numbers, outdoor processions and great joy. 'Thanks be to God' wrote Paul in 2 Corinthians 2:14, 'who in Christ always leads us in triumph and through us spreads the fragrance of the knowledge of him everywhere.' That remains part of the church's calling, and it calls for training, though much is also spontaneous!

6. *Overall church training.* We tried to do this in a variety of ways. One was by having carefully planned courses of sermons: sometimes topical, sometimes following the Church's year, sometimes expository. We tried to be sensitive to what the needs were at the time. Gradually we learnt how foolish we were to dart from subject to subject each week. We need to go on teaching on a particular topic until it is learnt and acted upon. With this in mind we organised a nine-month course, examining what it meant to be an alternative society in a world that is falling apart. We spent a whole month on each of nine aspects of this theme, and teaching took place at all levels in the church. The team preached on each topic for a whole month. The Fellowship Groups and prayer meetings discussed its application. Slide-tape sequences were produced on each topic. And we even made a loose-leaf guide book to the whole nine-month series, with opportunities for members to add material of their own.

The contents of this course may be of interest. The writer to the Hebrews shows how in a time when so much that seemed settled is being shaken, the church should exhibit qualities which belong to a lifestyle that cannot be shaken (Heb. 12:25–29). The marks of such a church are acceptable worship (12:28f; 13:15); love for the brethren (13:1); love for strangers (13:2) – which includes and should always accompany evangelism; love for the underprivileged (13:3); Christian family life (13:4); a simple lifestyle (13:5,6,16); spiritual leadership (13:7,17); sound teaching (13:9); and suffering (13:10–14) which is bound to be the badge of the faithful church, just as it was of the suffering Servant, her Lord.

The leadership of disciples

If a church is to engage in a servant ministry of mission and discipleship, this puts a great deal of responsibility upon the leadership. It is not surprising that in the New Testament Christian ministry is always shared ministry! No one person could or should undertake such an extensive ministry. It may be worth recounting how we have tried to go about building a leadership team.

The leadership of the church

The leadership in St. Aldate's had three constituent parts. First there was the staff. Second there was the Parochial Church Council, and more especially its Standing Committee; and thirdly there was a small group of men and women in the church who had shown pastoral gifts and were designated as a group of lay pastors. This diversification had great value, though it sometimes took a little time to pass a decision of importance through all three, especially since the church looked for a common mind led by the Lord, and eschewed voting. But it meant that there was a recognised pastoral group in the church to

141

whom people could turn as well as to the clergy. It meant that the leadership was shared between them on the pastoral side, and the P.C.C. on the worship and financial side, in addition to the ordained staff. And as some members were on two or, exceptionally, all three of those groups, it made for cohesion.

Lay pastors

What, you may ask, are lay pastors? Members of the congregation whom God has clearly gifted for leadership in the church. What do they do? They each have a responsibility for a few Fellowship Group leaders. They meet with them regularly to see how their groups are going, and to give encouragement and help as they are able. But lay pastors have other responsibilities too. They often share in the leading of worship; they may take the first part of the service, or lead the prayers, or speak. Some of the pastors showed gifts of evangelism, some of training, and these were appreciated and used. We found that pastors grew into taking teams out to different churches in the vicinity, either to run a day conference embodying a number of seminars on different aspects of the faith, or to take services over a weekend. Occasionally one of them would go overseas with a team, in answer to an invitation. Sometimes a member of the ordained staff went with such a group, but this became increasingly unnecessary. The lay pastors were well able to exercise the leadership themselves. Is this not an indication of the type of training which would be invaluable for Auxiliary Pastoral Ministry and for Lay Readers within the Anglican Church – and other Churches? Would it not give that element of practical experience within a team of like-minded partners, which is at present so lacking in their largely bookish training? The church at large tends to make a big mistake

with its people: they are generally given financial
and administrative jobs. While these need to be done,
it is important to involve people in the teaching,
pastoral and evangelistic ministry of the church. In
this way they develop fast, and the church develops
with them.

We found that it was imperative to keep the lay pastors in close contact both with the Fellowship Group
leaders on the one hand and with the ordained staff
on the other. Accordingly, we met for worship and
breakfast fortnightly, and had one evening a month
as pastors and another as pastors and spouses all
together. In this way the pastors came very close to
one another, and were able to share at a deep level;
moreover they actually modelled that type of close
fellowship which they hoped to inculcate throughout
the congregational groups over which they exercised
oversight.

But where, you may ask, do these pastors spring
from? The answer is simple. They are those who
have shown pastoral gifts. When people display gifts
of leadership and shepherding in the congregation
they may well be called to this work. Some of them
will have been Fellowship Group leaders, but not all.
Some will have displayed pastoral gifts in other areas.
By becoming pastors these people are released from
other responsibilities in the church and enabled to use
their gift for the Body as a whole.

They are set aside for this work in a service slightly
reminiscent of an ordination. Just as the bishop shares
his cure of souls with the incumbent, so the incumbent
shares it with them, publicly in the face of the congregation. We at St. Aldate's asked pastors to serve for
a renewable period of one year. Thus if other work
becomes pressing, if a wrong choice has been made,
or if the person moves away, the annual nature of

the appointment gives room for adjustment. We tried to follow the New Testament precedent of asking the congregation to suggest names, from which the existing leadership selected after prayerfully coming to a common mind.

Shared leadership

Leadership in New Testament days was shared. Whether you look at the twelve apostles of Jesus, or the 'prophets and teachers' in the church of Antioch (Acts 13:1), or the five types of ministry characterised as Christ's gift to the church (Eph. 4:11), the message is the same: Christian leadership is both servant leadership and shared leadership. It abominates both domination and monarchy. But monarchy is so much easier than shared leadership. There is therefore a strong tendency for us to relapse into an authoritarian stance when the pressures are on. How can this be avoided, and shared leadership be made to work? The following suggestions are not exhaustive, but they are certainly rooted in experience – much of it painful.

1. *We must acknowledge the Lordship of Jesus.* That is to say, we must recognise that the local church is not a monarchy, to be run by the rector. It is not an oligarchy, to be dominated by Parish Council or pastoral group. It is not a democracy, to be controlled by the congregation at large. The church is a theocracy. God created it, redeemed it, owns and controls it. It is his will that we must seek and be willing to follow. Therefore when we disagree on some matter we must neither try to force our view on others, nor weakly give way to them. We must argue the case as clearly and forcibly as we can. We must then go away and pray; and go on praying until we come to

a common mind. The way of the world is to vote.
But that leaves a dissatisfied minority. The way of
the Lord is to seek his face. When all want his will
even more than their own ideas, he does make his way
known. It may come through acceptance of the original
majority view. It may come through recognition that
the original minority view was right. It may come
through some totally new insight. We have seen it
come at times through a vision and at times through
a prophetic message from one member which so had
the ring of truth about it that all were convinced –
and subsequent events showed the correctness of the
decision. God will not guide us unless we deeply
desire to go his way at all costs. In St. Aldate's
we found that unitive guidance came most readily
after an extended period of worship and prayer.
This could happen spontaneously in the course of
a church business meeting – or perhaps during a
special day given over to prayer and fasting and
seeking the will of God for the church.

2. *We must listen to the church.* It is all too easy for
the leadership of a church to get out of step with the
membership. Instead of equipping the church members for their God-given ministries, the leadership
pursues its own ideas. This can cause disunity and
even disintegration in a congregation. But it can be
avoided. We tried to do this in two ways. First, we
kept in constant touch with the feelings and priorities
of church members through the Fellowship Group
system. Each of the lay pastors related to three or four
Fellowship Group leaders, and met them regularly.
They also visited the Fellowship Groups from time
to time. Two way communication was thus made
easy. The other way was to have a shortened Sunday service occasionally, followed by a congregational

discussion of some issue that was causing concern – and doing it within the context of worship, prayer, and openness. In ways such as these, together with the occasional questionnaire and written explanation of recent decisions taken by the leadership, it was usually possible to ensure that no substantial division emerged in the Body. Often there was truth on both sides of a controversial issue, but the proportions had gone awry. Then the guidance of the congregation at large was of tremendous value in restoring balance.

3. *We must recognise each other's gifts.* All leadership in the church is a gift of Christ. Therefore we do well to discern what those gifts are, in the leadership as well as in the congregation as a whole, and set each person free to use that gift for the good of the Body. 1 Corinthians 12:4–6 has wise advice for us. We have all been baptised into the same Body, and the Spirit of God has gifted every member. His goals are diversity, but harmony. And three key words are used by Paul to help the Corinthians understand their gifts. The first is *charisma*: each member has received some gracious endowment by the Lord. These are varied, and not subject to human manipulation. The second word is *diakonia*: the gifts are not intended for show but for service. They are meant to build up the Body in some appropriate way. The third word is *energema*: these gifts should be exercised not in our strength but the Lord's. That is how God's gifts are meant to fuse together for the good of the whole Body.

If we accept this, it will have costly consequences. It will mean that vicars may not do all the preaching – or even most of it, if they have not been particularly gifted as teachers, and others have been. They may have to yield to others in evangelism, or administration, or counselling. My wife was a much better counsellor than I: so she took the lead in this area of our ministry. Some of my colleagues were much better at planning worship, chairing meetings, looking after the staff team than I. So they did it. I was ultimately accountable to the congregation and to the bishop for the way these matters were handled; the buck stopped on my desk. But this does not mean that I attempted to head up the various aspects of our church's life. In most cases I worked *under* some other member of the team (over which I presided) because God had manifestly gifted him or her more than me in that area. Ministry is, after all, a matter of function, not of status. But we will still find that a hard lesson to learn: at least, I do! Yet how worthwhile when we succeed in freeing one another to exercise our gifts without thought of status or seniority. Then the Body is built up, and sees at the centre of its life a model for ministry.

4. *We must reciprocate ministry to one another.* Traditionally this is not the way we operate. Ministry is usually expected to flow one way, from the pastor to the people. But who looks after the pastors? Who listens to their aches? How do they keep fresh? Again, the traditional answers have been for the clergy to keep a stiff upper lip and pretend they have no problems. Or to look to a friend or confessor outside the parish. Or to rely on an occasional retreat. But how much better to have a fellowship of leadership within the parish, where joys and sorrows can be shared, and rebukes given and accepted in love.

The pastoral leadership in St. Aldate's had many shortcomings, but it proved its worth abundantly in reciprocal ministry. We have had many hilarious times together. I believe that we have all, on occasion, broken down and wept. Certainly I have been more ministered to than I have ministered in such a group. I have been wonderfully sustained and painfully rebuked. Members have loved me enough to tell me my faults, and to help me come to terms with them. Rebuke like this is costly to give, and costly to receive. But it makes for growth. I would hate to go back to the old way of apparent invulnerability and pretended competence. I know I am a weak and sinful man: I need my close partners in leadership to help me grow and to offset my inadequacies and stupidities.

Such community of leadership is rare, but it need not be. It can happen anywhere. All that is needed is for ordained ministers to gather round them small groups of committed Christians who will love and disciple one another. They can pour themselves into such groups. They share much of their lives together. Financial, ministerial, personal, matrimonial issues can be worked over together. All are enriched. And the pattern of servant leadership begins to emerge.

Enabling leadership

It is one thing to recognise that the function of Christian leadership is to equip members of the congregation for their ministry. It is quite another actually to do it. How can we enable people to discover their gifts, and use them for the common good?

1. *We can equip by teaching*. It is deeply entrenched in the mind of the average Christian that ministry is the role of the paid professional. Therefore constant teaching on the importance and usefulness of every limb in the Body is essential. The leadership needs repeatedly to expose the congregation to the biblical truth that all, and not some, Christians are ministers of Christ. It is unfortunately so revolutionary a concept that it will take time to get assimilated.

2. *We can equip by modelling.* It is no good vicars preaching every member ministry if they persist in doing everything of significance in the church. To be sure, many parishioners will not feel they have been visited if the vicar does not come in person. But the vicar will be doing them a long-term service by training a team of lay visitors who can effectively cover a small area regularly and build up relationships with those in their street, particularly if the visiting is seen as the responsibility of the Fellowship Group in the area. Members of the congregation may well be shocked to find the vicar sitting in the pew occasionally, and a lay leader taking the Sunday service. But they will see that every member ministry is being taken very seriously. We must not only teach, but demonstrate that the church does not consist of one member but many; that all are called to serve; and that a number are called to lead.

3. *We can equip by discipling.* Jesus did this with the twelve, and more intensively with Peter, James and John. Barnabas did it with Saul of Tarsus. He and Saul did it with John Mark – and so did Simon Peter. John had a school of disciples around him in Ephesus. The craftsmen of the Middle Ages each had their group of apprentices. And yet this method of encouraging gifts and ministries is strangely neglected in the modern church. Paul charged Timothy, his own erstwhile apprentice, 'what you have heard from me among many witnesses entrust to faithful men who will be able to teach others also' (2 Timothy 2:2). It is highly effective in producing the next generation of leaders, as many of the para-church organisations like Navigators and even sects like Mormons have been quick to recognise.

4. *We can equip by exposure.* People frequently have no idea of their gifts until they are exposed to some situation, and encouraged to launch out. I think of a gifted young evangelist who had no idea he possessed such a gift until he brought someone to me and asked me to show him the way to a living faith. I said, 'No: you are his friend. You show him.' He did, and he has been doing it ever since. I think of someone with a gentle singing voice. 'I could never sing a solo in church,' she felt. But one day she launched out in faith. God used her: and she now has a real ministry in song. I think of a group of young people who launched out into leading the prayers one night in church. It showed them they could lead people much older than themselves. I think of a man with a budding prophetic gift. Once the plunge was taken and he had spoken, however hesitantly, in church, he developed rapidly. And I think of my own life. I know that I have grown most when I have been thrust into situations where I had to attempt some sort of ministry though aware I was totally ill-equipped for it. We get equipped by exposure.

In his remarkable book *Dedication and Leadership*, Douglas Hyde, communist turned Christian, has this to say:

> The instruction of a new Party member does not normally begin immediately after he joins. Quite deliberately, and with good reason, the Party sends its new members, wherever possible, into some form of public activity *before instruction begins*.[1]

This is precisely the principle adopted by Jesus. He told Peter to follow him in order to become a fisher of men. His 'come and see' invitation was followed by 'go and tell'. Jesus sent out his disciples to tell others long before they were ready, by our standards. They learned fast, as they engaged in practical service.

How unlike the modern church, where large numbers gather and listen to one person exercising a preaching gift, while the vast majority passively listen (or slumber). Seldom is anyone trusted with any ministry until they have been Christians for some years and proved themselves. Little is expected of new Christians until they have sat and listened and grown enough to mature. What fools we are! It is hard to imagine how a church structure could be better designed to frustrate initiative and discourage the gifts of members than the structures common to our mainline denominations. By contrast, the new believers at Thessalonica were left to fend for themselves and provide their own incipient leadership a mere three weeks after being evangelised by Paul. That is exactly how the gospel has spread so fast among the Quichua Indians of Colombia in recent years: the converts were entrusted with leadership. Indeed, all over the Third World, church growth, under young and supposed ill trained leaders, has long surpassed that in Europe and the United States!

5. *We can equip by means of house groups.* The group in the home is a superb place to discover and encourage the gifts and ministries of church members. In the intimacy of the home group people will venture into an area of ministry which they would never attempt in public. It may be letter writing to a missionary, or playing a guitar in worship, or making the supper for the group. It is important to encourage everyone to undertake some activity in the group. Indeed, encouragement in general is of the utmost importance. 'We know in part and we prophesy in part' wrote Paul (1 Cor. 13). He might well have added that *all* our

gifts and ministries are partial and imperfect. People need to be encouraged to experiment, and to accept instruction and, if necessary, correction. 'Trust God, and have a try' is much better advice than 'Attempt nothing unless you are sure you can do it.' It is not only prophecy, but every other gift that needs to be exercised 'according to the measure of faith' (Rom. 12:3). This lays on Christian leaders the responsibility of creating a climate of expectation that God will use the most unlikely people, and of willingness for mistakes to be made and accepted in love. When people feel secure, then they are prepared to experiment. It is in this way that they generally discover what are and what are not their gifts.

At least once a year it is good to have an evening when members share what they would really love to do in Christ's service. Our own spiritual desires are often an indication of potential gifts. Another evening should be given to affirming one another. 'What I most appreciate about you is . . .' Often people are astonished to discover gifts in this way. And gifts discovered and tested in the small group may subsequently become important to the church at large. Whether they do or not, the member concerned has found a ministry, and the leadership has fulfilled its role by helping to bring this about.

6. *We can equip by involvement*. Everyone who is doing anything in the church should be equipped to do it better. And everyone who has received training should be given a sphere in which to exercise it. These are two aspects of training by involvement which are crucial to hold together.

St. Aldate's Church was no expert in all this. Looking back on those challenging and exciting years I am all too well aware that we did not equip all active members of our church to exercise their gifts better. We often failed to use them in 'hands on' experience after they had been trained. However we profited a great deal from an annual training course. It took an evening a week for three months. It included two full Saturday conferences, and was followed by a weekend of ministry in a nearby parish, when teams of those who had been on the course went out with their tutors to serve local churches that were often small and struggling. It was a tremendous encouragement to local Christians and visitors alike. In recent years the course has been run on a Deanery level, and wider. It has lost something in intimacy and depth, perhaps, but it has gained enormously by servicing Christian people from a wide variety of churches within a twenty mile radius.

The course is by invitation only, and can be run either by the parish staff or, better, on a local ecumenical basis. Each evening consists of a time of worship, led by the participants; a time of sustained teaching; coffee or a meal; and the last part of the evening in tutor groups, where the topic may be tackled by guided discussion, role-play, or some other method. Each member of the group spends two personal sessions with the tutor, and is put through his paces by means of a 'dry run' of counselling, of personal evangelism, and of handling some great subject like suffering, with an imaginary enquirer. Each member of the group will speak under supervision at some church gathering, however small. And during the weekend away, some will lead a service, some pray or give testimony in public, some lead a house group, some address teenagers. Often an evangelistic address brings the mini-mission to an end, and that gives the chance for members of the course to counsel enquirers and help them through to assurance in Christ. Needless to say, many gifts emerge and much growth takes place on a course like this. It leads on to various other small courses: on controversial doctrinal issues, on public speaking, on counselling and on the leadership of small groups, especially Fellowship Groups.

Many congregations will feel that they are unable to mount anything of the sort. Many clergy will feel that they do not have that type of talent in their church. I have a suspicion that both are wrong. The Lord gives gifts to his church, and those gifts include the various ministries we have been talking of (Eph. 4:11,12). If we doubt this, we doubt the Lord.

Management or ministry?

In the vast majority of churches the models of ministry are frankly managerial, if they exist at all. The ordained minister is the acknowledged leader of the enterprise. Sometimes there is a parish assistant, a secretary or a curate. But the vicar is in the driving seat. That is what training was all about. That is what the congregations have been trained to expect. Can such ingrained attitudes change? Is the model of servant leadership, demonstrated and required by Jesus, too threatening, too demanding?

Change is certainly possible, if all concerned are prepared to pay the price. It is really a matter of attitude. If the minister even in a small country parish is gripped by the New Testament vision of every limb in the Body working properly and making its own special contribution, then it can happen. It lies very much in the hands of the ordained clergy. To be sure, they may have to counteract the weight of tradition. They may have to go against 'what has always been done'. But if they believe that all are called to serve, if they believe that the presbyterate should consist of

154

a team rather than an individual, if they believe that the potential for Christian ministry lies slumbering there in the pews waiting to be mobilised, they can act: indeed they must. And they do not need to wait for changes in the laws of the Church.

I know of no Church law to prevent the rector gathering a group of people with whom to share the oversight of the congregation. I know of no Church law to prevent training courses figuring strongly in the programme of a church, so that the saints are built up for service. I know of no Church law to prevent men and women within the congregation from sharing in leading the worship, the evangelism, the teaching, the counselling, the house groups and from assisting in administering the Holy Communion. Why should the vicar chair the Parochial Church Council or indeed the church staff meeting? I do not chair either of them. There are others better able to do it. Let them exercise their ministry for the good of the bodies concerned. Why should the rector administer the parish if there are others with greater organisational skills to do so? Why should we not form a mixed leadership team of men and women, ordained and lay within our parishes? I know of no reason except for inertia, inherited prejudice and fear.

Perhaps fear is the strongest of these; fear that it might be too radical, fear that the incumbent would not have anything left to do, fear of the invasion of cherished areas of monopoly. In point of fact these fears are groundless. Perfect love casts out fear, and when that love runs throughout the Body such fears are wont to disappear. It may be radical to encourage the gifts of all within the priestly Body of Christ; but it is biblical, and it works. It only seems radical because we have been disobedient so long. And as for the fear that the trained person, the vicar, will be

unemployed if others are equipped to minister, this
does not happen. They will cover far more ground
between them than a single person ever could. Ministers will therefore be faced with more problems and
be called upon for more guidance in more lively and
challenging situations than they have ever known
before. Moreover, since they have donned the apron
of the Servant, they will see that others in leadership
teams don it too. No longer will they be isolated. They
will find themselves in the centre of loving teams of
servants. Others will serve them, just as they serve
others. And the pattern of the supreme Servant will
increasingly be seen in such congregations.

Is it too much to hope that some such manifestation
of Servant ministry be widely seen in our Church in
this country, before persistence in the present models
of expensive professionalism in diminishing congregations brings our beloved Church to bankruptcy and
perhaps to dissolution? More than once in previous
generations God has had to break what would not
bend. Pray God it may not be so with us! He need
not, if we apply the scriptural model of the Servant to
this the most controversial and resistant of all areas
within the church, her ordained ministry.

REFERENCES

Chapter 2
1. O. Cullmann, *The Christology of the New Testament*, S.C.M., p. 161.
2. J. Jeremias, *The Servant of God*, S.C.M., p. 98f.
3. T.W. Manson, *The Church's Ministry*, Hodder, p. 27.

Chapter 3
1. E. Brunner, *The Misunderstanding of the Church*, Lutterworth, p. 50.
2. M. Harper, *Let My People Grow*, Hodder.
3. J.B. Lightfoot, *The Christian Ministry*, Thynne and Jarvis, p. 5.
4. *Ibid*, p. 5.

Chapter 4
1. B.L. Manning, *A Layman in the Ministry*, Independent Press, p. 152.
2. D. Daube, *The New Testament and Rabbinic Judaism*, London, p. 244ff.
3. J. Jeremias, *Zeitschrift für die neutestamentlich Wissenschaft*, 1957, p. 130f.
4. Hugh Silvester, *The Theology of Ordination*, an unpublished paper.
5. Hans Küng, *Why Priests?*, Fontana, p. 67.

6. M. Harper, *op. cit.* p. 230.
7. E. Brunner, *op. cit.* chs. 7–10.
8. E. Schweizer, *Church Order in the New Testament*, S.C.M., p. 186.

Chapter 5
1. Cranmer, *Remains and Letters*, p. 305.
2. Hooper, *Later Writings*, p. 90.
3. Lightfoot, *op. cit.* p. 22.

Chapter 6
1. W. Telfer, *The Office of a Bishop*, D.L.T., p. 41.
2. A.T. Hanson, *The Pioneer Ministry*, S.C.M., p. 144.
3. *Christianity Divided*, ed. D.J. Callahan, Sheed and Ward, p. 10.
4. See Cullmann's chapter 'The Tradition' in his *The Early Church*, S.C.M.
5. A. Ehrhardt, *The Apostolic Succession*, Lutterworth, p. 20.
6. See his article 'Apostle' in the Kittel *Wörterbuch zum Neuen Testament*.
7. This is acknowledged by Dix in *The Apostolic Ministry*, ed. K.E. Kirk, Hodder, p. 200.
8. Kirk in *The Apostolic Ministry*, p. 40.
9. See E. Molland in the *Journal of Ecclesiastical History*, 1950, i, p. 12ff.
10. See W. Telfer in the *Journal of Ecclesiastical History*, 1952, iii, p. 1f.
11. T.M. Lindsay, *The Church and the Ministry in the Early Centuries*, Hodder, p. 279.
12. W. Telfer, *The Office of a Bishop*, D.L.T., p. 119.
13. Richard Hooker, *Ecclesiastical Polity*, 7.5.8, and 7.14.11.
14. This is extensively documented in Norman Sykes, *Old Priest and New Presbyter*, C.U.P.
15. Cited by N. Sykes, *op. cit.* p. 212.

References

Chapter 7

1. A.G. Hebert, *Ways of Worship*, cited in Lambeth Report (1958) 2.85.
2. Alan Richardson, *Introduction to the Theology of the New Testament*, S.C.M., p. 201.
3. *Ibid*, p. 303.
4. Lightfoot, *op. cit.* p. 123ff., Lindsay, *op. cit.* p. 308, Tertullian, *De Baptismo*, 5.
5. Chrysostom, *Homily on Hebrews*, 13.8.
6. This doctrine evoked John Knox's protest: 'Is there any oblivion or forgetfulness fallen on God the Father? Hath he forgotten the death and passion of Jesus Christ, so that he needs to be brought in memory thereof by any mortal man?'
7. B.F. Westcott, *The Epistle of the Hebrews*, Macmillan, p. 230.
8. Justin, *Dialogue*, 41.
9. Lightfoot, *op. cit.* p. 134.
10. Cranmer, *The Lord's Supper*, Thynne, v. 11.
11. *Ibid.* v. 3.
12. Hooker, *op. cit.* v. 78.

Chapter 8

1. See Clement of Alexandria, *Stromateis*, 3.18.
2. *Women and Holy Orders*, p. 126.

Chapter 9

1. See Ronald Higgins, *The Seventh Enemy*, Hodder.

Chapter 10

1. Douglas Hyde, *Dedication and Leadership*, Notre Dame, p. 42.

159